Painting the
LANDSCAPE
OF
LONELINESS

OLIVIA ASH, ESQ., MS

Painting the
LANDSCAPE
OF
LONELINESS

THE DRIVE TO CONNECT AND THE
STRATEGIES TO IDENTIFY YOUR NEEDS

Visit the author's website at www.livbalanced.net

Published and distributed by Merack Publishing
San Diego, USA
www.merackpublishing.com

Cover Artwork & Content Illustrations by Olivia Ash except facing Page 1 by @simplysophiedesigns

Library of Congress Control Number: 2023920902
Ash, Olivia
Painting the Landscape of Loneliness: The Drive to Connect and The Strategies to Identify Your Needs

ISBNs 978-1-957048-91-8 (Paperback)
978-1-957048-93-2 (eBook)

Disclaimer

This book is neither legal nor medical advice. I wrote it to canvas the various ways loneliness reveals itself through human experience. Life is hard; sometimes, we simply need to talk about how we feel and know another is listening without judgment. If you are a U.S. resident and need support; are in crisis; or feel upset, scared, or distressed, text SHARE to 741741 for free, confidential crisis counseling.

Dedication

Reader: you are not alone in feeling lonely. It means you are human.

May the interplay of research and memory
paint a story that resonates with you.

Contents

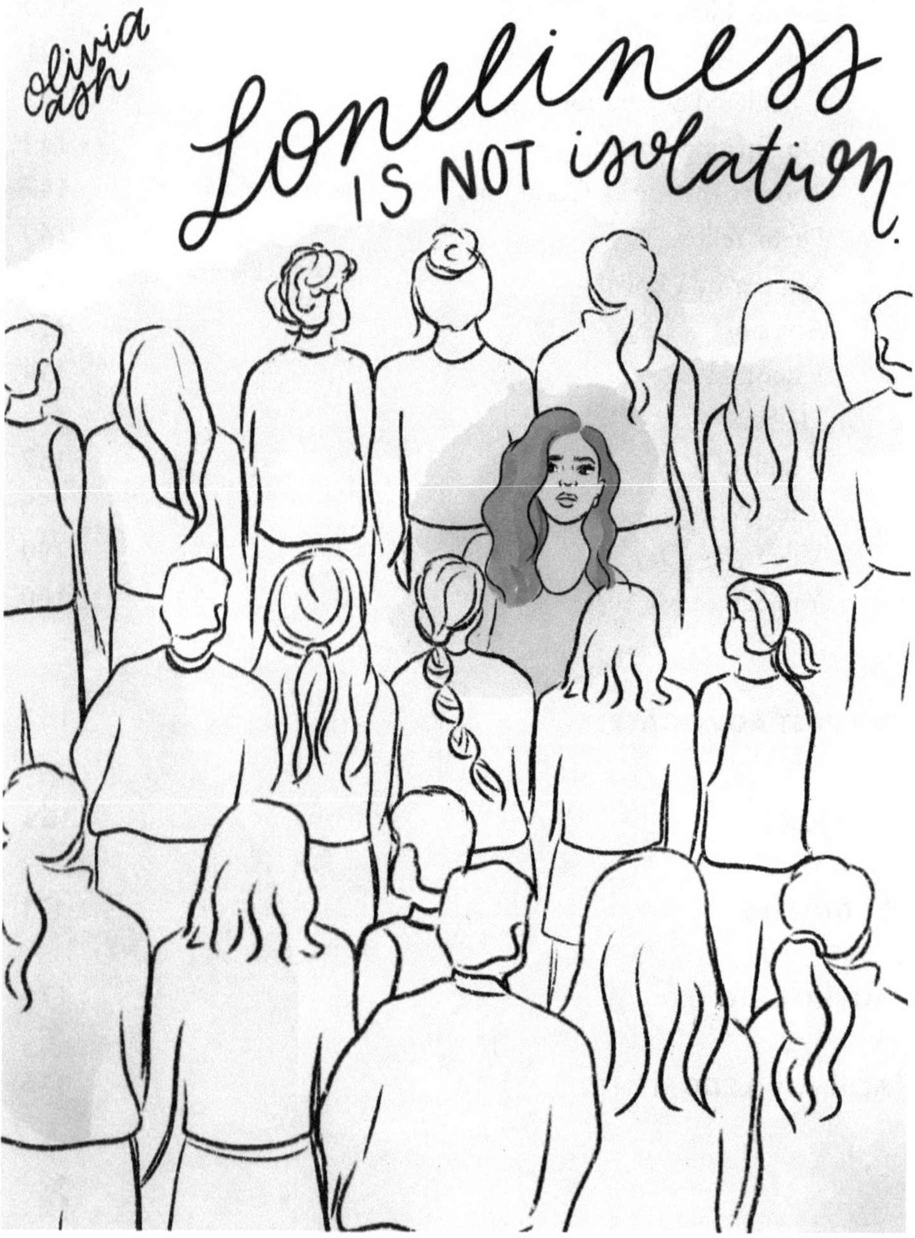
olivia cash
Loneliness IS NOT isolation.

INTRODUCTION

IF SHOWERS COULD TALK
Indianapolis, Indiana

I want to hold space for the place where you *break down* and where you break-it-down. Where your body shakes as visceral outcries emerge from the depth of your chest. Where you permit yourself to crumble and experience the breakdown you never want anyone to witness—not even your closest friends and family. This space contains exploding emotions that shock your awareness with profound arrogance. Wherein the morning after your abdomen aches from gymnastics-like grieving and your eyelids swell from the torrent of tears. Where you scream and cry until nothing is left, and then cry again. I want to canvas the place where your essence teeters on the brink of complete disintegration yet remains surefooted. Do you know that place? I want to *honor* that space. Because in that space is where we meet our true self with its wounds and wins. In this safe space, my soul unravels with the fury of a thousand tsunamis. If life has yet to bring you to the space where emotional thunderbolts astonish and rivers of grief swell—wait. I have such a place; do you?

Nobody wants to talk about the hard things, but the hard things must be discussed. Nobody wants to dive too deeply into their emotions, let alone into the depths of loneliness. Our lonely feelings are too vulnerable to expose to subversive whispers and ridicule. So, we simply ignore loneliness and don't speak of its shameful weakness. Instead, our hyper-independent society urges us to smile while repressing a scream and stoically state, "I can do it by myself." Between culture, rearing, and experience, we hear, "Be strong. Eliminate weakness. If you feel icky, stuff those feelings and act as though they don't exist. Be positive!"

If, oftentimes, we reveal our emotions, we are branded as "too emotional" or "too sensitive." And what about loneliness? If we acknowledge IT lurking in the recesses of our soul, then we must be flawed. Though it's an emotion, like all others, somehow admitting to loneliness means we are "broken," and that's just sad. And nobody wants to be sad, right? Only positive vibes here.

Let's get real and face the hard things. We are not automatons; we are humans. We ebb and flow. We are both weak and strong. Instead of shunning, stuffing, or storing loneliness, let's bring it to the forefront. That's where it belongs. We cool the burning within by acknowledging, listening, and learning from loneliness. It cannot be eliminated; it is. And this is by design; it exists as a guide. When we make space for it, the pressure of loneliness lessens. The more often we heed its call, the more we align with our essence and the burdens lessen. Loneliness may be subtle and slow growing, or acute and profound. Loneliness is a force of nature that drives us to seek life because it alerts us to what is missing, and to seek solace in community. It can powerfully change perspective and rearrange priorities. Listen to its alarm and heed its caution. In doing so, you'll appease its appetite and ease the ache.

"Loneliness is such a painful, frightening experience that people will do everything to avoid it."

~ Freda Fromm Reichmann

DICKINSON AND ME

Meaning is what you make it.

I can't explain my curiosity, like gravity, towards Emily Dickinson's poetry as a young woman. Her poetry surfaced through the soil of my life, season after season, with apparent random purpose. Now, thirty years later, circumstances reveal a serendipitous alignment. I hear the dissonance resolving into a beautiful chord and see the chaotic cloud of confusion evaporate with the heat of morning's sunlight, revealing a clear scene. I sense meaning, harmony, and balance. In two of her poems, as if in a mirror, I see my innermost soul reflected.

The first poem, *VI*, reflects how my inner child feels towards humanity. It's printed on a well-worn page in my volume of her *Collected Poems*,[1] quietly appreciated on the shelf.

VI

by Emily Dickinson

If I can stop one heart from breaking,
I shall not live in vain;
If I can ease one life the aching,
Or cool one pain,
Or help one fainting robin
Unto his nest again,
I shall not live in vain.

The second poem, *The Loneliness One dare not sound (Poem 777),* is no less profound, though perhaps more mysterious. This poem is brilliant, even more so to my eyes after years of living, researching, and speaking about loneliness. Within its riddle-like stanzas lie, I believe, the means to manage and mitigate our own lonely feelings. Irony slapped me in the face at the knowledge that Emily lived her days as a recluse in her family home. Sustained in the essentials—ample food and warm shelter—her soul survived on breadcrumbs. The daughter of a lawyer, she attempted connection with the outside world, but ultimately lived life in a silent cavern, loneliness her constant companion.

THE LONELINESS ONE DARE NOT SOUND (777)²

by Emily Dickinson

The Loneliness One dare not sound—
And would as soon surmise
As in its Grave go plumbing
To ascertain the size—

The Loneliness whose worst alarm
Is lest itself should see—
And perish from before itself
For just a scrutiny—

The Horror not to be surveyed—
But skirted in the Dark—
With Consciousness suspended—
And Being under Lock—

I fear me this—is Loneliness—
The Maker of the soul
Its Caverns and its Corridors
Illuminate—or seal—

Much like the character of Joy awakens to Sadness' critical importance in life within the animated film *Inside Out*, we must accept that loneliness serves a purpose. It should have a place card at the table with Joy, Anger, Sadness, Fear, and Love—with Like and Dislike.[3] It is important too. We must embrace what Emily Dickinson described[4] as the "horror not to be surveyed" and the "maker of the soul." We must befriend Loneliness.

Befriend it? Emily so feared loneliness that she, arguably one of America's greatest poets, described it as The Maker of our souls. Definitions for the soul vary and are as varied as people, but I fancy this one: "the principle of life, feeling, thought, and action in humans."[5] I regard our soul, our *animating principle,* as our mind, will, and emotions. She further described loneliness as a *horror* to be avoided and skirted in the dark. A *horror* is "an overwhelming and painful feeling caused by something frightfully shocking, terrifying, or revolting."[6] Is loneliness revolting? Emily banishes it from the Mt. Olympus of Emotions, unfit to coexist with other human emotions. It's a *shuddering fear.*[7] Yet, we know from research that loneliness plays an integral part in the drama of what it means to live human. Emily urges us not to measure it—to go around it instead. Loneliness, therefore, becomes the elephant in the room, the thorn we can't remove, the bastardized emotion we ignore. Yet loneliness is ever-present and must be digested, like an elephant, a bite at a time.

Talk about it we must—and this is why nobody wants to talk about It. Humans are masters at ignoring emotions that require an audience. We are proficient at numbing our souls with instant gratification while dissonance grows like mildew in the depths of our psyche. I'll leave psychology to the licensed professionals, yet I know this to be true. Why do we ignore what requires exposure to fresh air and light? I believe a reason is that we've poorly learned to listen—to truly listen—and sit with our emotions in a safe and supportive space.

I'm not a psychologist, psychiatrist, or a medical doctor. I don't pretend to be a philosopher or spiritual guide. I am, however, a lifelong learner. I create. I paint, sketch, and write. Nature and movement are my mentors and healers. I'm an art-loving attorney and teacher of well-being, movement science, and biology. I've learned lessons in my forty-three years of living, loving, and losing. I'm also a human doing what I can with what I have, learning to radically accept the perfectly imperfect existence we call life.

To *live human* means to experience technicolor emotions, including loneliness. I'm no exception to life's lessons. I've learned to listen to my Lonely through research and living—through both pleasures and pains. And this is why I want to share—to pull back the curtain on a mystery and reveal—as though I was Dorothy in the Land of Oz at the Emerald City—that loneliness is not a scary overlord. It's part of us. Loneliness exists to guide us to experiencing the most from our unique existence. It urges us to connect to others; to better understand who we are, what we need, and what we want. We are each doing what we can with what we have, right now. Let's allow loneliness to be what it is—a human emotion that exists to reveal how capable we are to feel deeply and profoundly. What we deem profound is unique to each of us. The journey of discovering this is where our Lonely is the teacher.

In a 2018 survey of American workers, lawyers rated the loneliest.

Liv Ash

I read an article in which a survey[8] stated that lawyers rated the loneliest of American workers. As a fourth-year law student, I wanted to learn reasons for this harrowing result. For my doctoral thesis, I applied my training in well-being to the study of law and specifically, law students. I conducted original research and, in the process, opened a Pandora's Box I've been sifting for five years.

This book beckoned for birth despite my attempts to stifle the calls. I submitted my thesis, graduated from law school, and began bar exam studies. Over the next two years, I busied myself with life, pouring energy into work and recovering from cranial surgery. Yet, on a cool October evening while cycling through the city, I heard the familiar call and listened to its weary groans (and groaned inwardly, knowing the energy it would require to share my story).

I decided to share my story anyway; revisit research; and write this book. I knew this topic required reliving painful memories, yet believed they would resonate with all. I believe we learn to live with loneliness by sharing our stories. Stories are powerful; how loneliness reveals itself in my life may be different from how it looks in another's life. Having journaled my heart out for a decade and completed research on loneliness, I knew most persons felt moderate (many severe) levels of loneliness. I wanted—and needed—to help. Stories are serendipitously situated to illustrate the characteristics of loneliness. I believe strength is built through vulnerability, yet it's counterintuitive to expose ourselves. We are designed to survive, yet must choose to thrive. This requires that we learn how to process vulnerabilities. Science reveals effort is necessary to become physically stronger through gradual exposure to stressors—so why would strengthening our emotional health be any less effort?

History shows us that stories are powerful; we need only look to oral traditions before written history, and then to books, movies, and television. This is my story. I've woven my memories among data to illustrate intangible concepts about loneliness. I've also included stories voluntarily submitted through a survey I created based on my 2019 research. Throughout this collection of memories, I've chosen not to use names to honor privacy and lived experience. Therefore, all males are referred to as "he/him/his" and females as "she/her/hers" unless noted.

Let's learn about loneliness together. We all feel life's battle scars. I'll share mine. We'll move from memory to memory. You'll read poems I scribbled in my dog-eared journal the past twenty years because they assist in painting my inner landscape. Peppered among my memories are participant-submitted stories and research rest stops. Here, you can stretch, refuel, and process. I asked my social media followers to voluntarily take an anonymous survey. No compensation was given for the submission. In addition to a few demographic questions, I asked one question:

> *Please describe a time in your life when you felt lonely.*
> *Explain as best you can how it felt. Describe the context;*
> *this may include your emotions, and the place, people, and*
> *events in your life at that time. Then, as best as you can*
> *recall, rate your loneliness at that time as low, moderate,*
> *or high.*

All submissions received are included within this book and set in a table-like format. I've included demographics about the participant and their response to the question, in their words, edited for grammar and clarity. Given that loneliness affects everyone, perhaps you will resonate with a participant's response. Demographics are useful to reveal patterns; research indicates loneliness affects specific populations and persons based on many factors, including age, race, ethnicity, sex, gender, culture, socioeconomic status, marital status, occupation, and personal experience. In addition to these factors, our personalities affect how we perceive life. This includes how we process experience and relate to others.

I'll be your guide through the research, and not "research" in the typical sense of the word. I've already written and published *that* research.[9] Appendix A contains a list of resources, including *that* research and where to find it if you want to read into the weeds. Through speaking about loneliness with friends and teaching others in professional settings since beginning this journey, I knew something was missing in the field. We need a resource that would "bridge the gap" to help people understand how to identify and manage loneliness. Given that nobody wants to talk about loneliness anyway, I knew that to reach a broader audience, I had to write the resource. I had to reframe loneliness and present it as what it is—one human emotion among many.

A goal in writing this book was to share my research in a way that everyone could understand. Loneliness is a human emotion. We all manage loneliness. I want a teen or retiree to pick up this book and learn more about the nature of loneliness, and hopefully, themselves. With that goal in mind, I've converted essentials from my research into graphics to illustrate concepts. A picture speaks a thousand words and conjures many emotions. And sometimes, a thousand words can paint a picture. I've also included Table A – 10 Types of Loneliness, a summary of an article that helped me to identify specific types and origins of loneliness in my own life. When I do summarize loneliness concepts with words, I've shared it via manageable, everyday language. Last, I've reworked one of my previously published essays, *Adverse Possession*,[10] canvassing my battle with chronic illness and the pains that accompany it. Chronic pain is a container holding buckets of loneliness I've lived throughout my life.

Ever the teacher, my hope is that by using different learning modalities, all readers may apply concepts to real-life scenarios. These sources, when weaved together, create a frame within which to paint the landscape of loneliness. And like artwork, I hope readers will see themselves reflected in the brushstrokes and know they are not alone. Loneliness may feel devastatingly oppressive at moments, yet within that burden lies a unique opportunity to learn about you. Listen to your Lonely. It's sensitive; it's raw. And it exists to bring cleansing and clarity. Loneliness is waiting for you to listen and reveal how you may better align your desires with reality to maintain balance and fully experience living.

I wrote this book for me. I wrote this book for my colleagues—those lost and those struggling with loneliness. I wrote this book for anyone who has felt, feels, and will feel lonely—even desperately so—as a tangible reminder that loneliness is not to be feared or "skirted in the dark" as Emily Dickinson penned. It is part of your experience. I wrote this book for you. Together, let's lean into our Lonely.

LOVE THE YOU THAT LIVES IN THE DARK

by Olivia Ash

Lean into your Lonely,
for you are not alone.

Life is lived in both shadow and light.
Observe the interplay.

Lonely ebbs and flows as the tide.
Invite her in.

She reveals where to grow.
Listen.

LIV
Indiana

AUGUST 22

"Liv, you were into everything." I was curious and full of energy, so I'm told. Yet, I know this to be true. I am curious and full of energy. I move and create. Like the Energizer Bunny, I "keep going." I don't earn gold stars for this quality; it is what I know. At times, I desperately wish I could relax. But it is, and I am. So, I work with it.

How do things work? What's behind the curtain? I crave to learn, dig deep, and understand the "why" and "how" of what interests me. I seek life because life creates. Life is to be lived, isn't it? Otherwise, what's the point?

Someone recently asked me what I think upon first waking. Without hesitation, I replied, "Let's do this."

THE HARD THINGS

- I've never known a day without thinking my body could improve.
- I fear gaining weight.
- Sometimes, I exercise solely to "balance" the calories I ate, like a math equation.
- I often don't feel like eating because I'm tired. My diet is restricted; it's exhausting to walk the aisles of the grocery and be reminded of everything you can't eat. Emotions and mental tapes play on repeat and wear me out. *If I eat it, I could bloat or cramp and then I'd feel discomfort. I don't like feeling heavy. I hate it when my clothes are tight. Blah, blah, blah.*
- If I could turn light energy into food like plants, I would. Then I wouldn't feel like a child when someone asked me if I had "eaten real food" that day. Then I wouldn't be mad at myself for playing along and laughing it off when I really wish they would never ask.

- If I could, I'd make everything more peaceful and sparkling.

- Textured fabrics, sequins, and paillettes make me happy.

- Taupe makes me sad.

- Responsibility can be a burden and a bore.

- Crooked artwork agitates me; I can't help but notice it. If it's crooked, that means no one's noticed, and may not care.

- Violence hurts my soul.

- I feel beauty and ignorance simultaneously.

- It's hard to "turn off" my engine of sensing.

- I awaken most mornings at 3 a.m., heart racing and head pounding, fearing whether I made the "right" decision.

- I wish I could be more present.

- Chronic pain is exhausting, empty, and relentless. It's lonely knowing others can't feel the pain that never goes away, so how can you possibly explain it to them? It's easier to remain quiet and manage it in silence.

- Hypervigilance is exhausting; I don't know how to stop it.

- I'm tired.

THE MEMORY

Indiana

She's squatting, hovering above the dry, mid-summer grass, engrossed in the task at hand. Completely absorbed, she works the dirt with purpose, oblivious to anything except releasing emotion through sensation. She's coping through creation. When you ask her what she's doing, she remains quiet and focused on the task. She doesn't look at you; she continues moving dirt with bare hands, digging holes, and trimming grass. The day is bright and sunny. A western breeze gently loosens wisps of blonde hair from her ponytail. She doesn't notice; she's peacefully engaged.

Here there is no yelling, crying, or confinement. Angry verbal jabs that shudder and stifle are absent. Sensing frustration, sadness, or disappointment, she feels Everyone's hurt within her chest. She wishes she could reach out with comfort when words berate an organic expression, yet she can only observe and ache within. She sighs resignation as her chest tightens. She can offer no assistance. As the dissonance grows, she must escape the pain. Nature calls to her to soothe the wounds, for She is the only presence capable of neutralizing animated energy.

THE HALLWAY
Indiana

SOMETIME IN THE 1990'S

She was stuck in the space between. To her left—four curious and confused souls. To her right—their makers. Like Gods on Mt. Olympus, they sparred—first striking, then retreating, then redoubling efforts for another round. She watched it play out, listening to the sounds of battle. Though not in the fight, she felt each wound as the Titans' weapons clashed. The narrow hallway did little to shield them from the sounds of dismantling personalities.

Helplessness oozed from every pore, her mind reeling as it worked the problem. No leverage. No options. No solutions. She merely watched as he hurled verbal insults and she deflected, clawing wildly with her own, like a lioness defending her cubs. Except the lioness was not shielding them; they were forgotten.

The eldest grappled with indecision, torn between two worlds. Does she act? If she entered the battle, she would suffer heavy casualties, and fuel the fire. But if she remained in the middle, she was safe. Observing it all, she scrambled to retrieve the shards of her soul, crushing beneath the fray.

SILENCE AS ACCEPTANCE

Indiana

SOMETIME IN THE 1990'S

I didn't want to do it, yet what were my options? Defy authority? Argue? Suffer the backlash? No thanks. Oftentimes, after an argument she would change her appearance—specifically, her hair. Whether it happened often or only felt that way to my young brain, I recall it in memory and feeling. It was her quickest way to relief, I suppose.

With trepidation and a hesitant hand, I shaved her head after the argument. I hated it; it wasn't my burden to bear. And yet, when backed into a corner, what could I choose? With empathy only experience can teach, I know she suffered in silence. Perhaps the sheer act of someone else shearing her head—thereby drastically changing her appearance and metaphorically cutting off the painful "dead weight"—brought relief.

But it wasn't silent suffering; it was a visceral scream played out against her own being, but not by her own hand. I suffered in silence. I didn't want to bear a burden that wasn't mine. At that moment I took into my own heart someone else's pain, though I had not yet lived enough life to fully feel its ramifications. The foreign pain festered and grew. With time, it weakened my own malnourished self-compassion.

PLAYED ON REPEAT

Indiana

THE 1990'S

"You have broad shoulders and thick thighs."

"Don't wear your hair down, it's too 'sexy'."

"You're bigger than most men."

"You have a booty."

"You intimidate men."

"You think like a man."

"You're too sensitive."

"You're too emotional."

"You can't watch that, it's ungodly."

"You can't listen to that, it's ungodly."

"It's not Christ-like."

"You choked."

"You could have done it better."

"I would have done it this way."

"You're like me."

"Why didn't you win?"

"If you don't do it, no one will."

"You must, I depend on you. You're the glue that holds us together."

"You're the only one I can talk to."

"I was only joking."

The mind
is the soil
in which
loneliness
grows.

Liv Ash

WHO WILL SAVE YOUR SOUL?

Indiana

THANKSGIVING WEEKEND, 1999

An object in motion will remain in motion until an outside force stops it.

I screamed on impact. My body hit the dashboard with a thud. The seatbelt sliced into my chest and shoulder with fury, and my head flopped like a Raggedy Ann doll. The image of inevitability burns within my mind's eye like the Eye of Sauron. I faintly recall my parents standing on the pavement in the strobing police lights. Stunned into a stupor, first responders accompanied me to the ambulance as the other driver walked alongside, asking with an arrogance I wish I could have slapped from his grubby face, "Why didn't you just drive around me into the ditch?" Fury ignited, yet now wasn't the time to speak my mind.

I didn't know where he was; was he okay?

I would endure the ambulance ride alone. A silent peace lingered like early morning fog. Perhaps it was shock. Tending to my vitals, I could hear talking, checking items off a list. I lay on the gurney, staring at the ambulance ceiling. It was a curious ride that rainy evening. I don't remember speaking anything profound, nor do I recall an excessive emotional release. Grayscale scenes played out in muffled silence.

My low back ached. After colliding with the semi-tractor trailer, my neck muscles felt like worn punching bags. No broken bones, but my battered body bore bruises and invisible burdens. Days later, imaging revealed disjointed neck vertebrae and torn ligaments. Within five years, I'd have two shoulder surgeries and two spinal surgeries to replace a damaged, degenerated lumbar disc. Thank God we drove the Jeep; had it been the Bug, we'd be dead.

A RUDE AWAKENING
Evansville, Indiana

WINTER 2000

Chest compacted and soul sour, I rolled over, staring into the faint light of early morning. The dull throbbing pain at the base of my skull that radiated into my shoulder intensified. Lately, pain and I had "made it official," and I wasn't ready for a relationship. I was a busy undergraduate, my days consumed with study, work, and sport. I had two jobs—the job at the mall, and the full-time job to perform as a Division I athlete (preferably with more wins than mistakes). I'd accomplished my high school goal: to earn a scholarship. It was either academics or sport, and sport offered me a full ride. Easy decision.

Yet, the body aches worsened; indeed, they rarely left. Whether in my neck, shoulder, back, or ankle, pain radiated. Tingling, throbbing, aching, popping pains consistently lapped upon me like the ocean upon the shore. Though the two-inch strip of nylon restrained me from catapulting through the windshield, it couldn't prevent the slamming of my knees into the console, or the wicked whiplash sustained as physics rendered my neck as supple as a Christmas goose. It had been a few months since colliding head-long into that jackknifed semi. Still alive and nineteen years young, I should feel grateful, but I did not. Dismayed, I stoked a fire of fitful anger.

The pressure of heated frustration ached within my chest, burning through the boundaries of my tender heart. I was broken in body and spirit. Brokenness brought shame and failure. They may as well have been Greece's Three Fates. I wept stinging tears of sadness and grief. I didn't know what to do. My plans for athletic success were evaporating before my eyes. My neck muscles burned. I swear, the sound of pain throbbing through my body was audible. Couldn't anyone else hear it too?

WRITE YOUR HEART OUT
Indiana

2001 – 2002

The first rule of journaling is to date your entries. Be specific. Begin with the five "Ws" : Who, What, When, Where, and Why.

ACHING
by Olivia Ash

JULY 8, 2001

Sometimes I feel like an old creaky chair.
Functioning, yet so worn by its functioning,
And the effects of wear and weather.
Plenty of life left, yet vigilant of deepening stress marks.
Fine, hairline ruts that beckon for attention,
Reminding the rocker of its limitations.
Slowly, so as not to bring acute pain,
I wear away,
Rusting without the fluid of vitality.
I settle into place to begin another day.

LONELINESS
by Olivia Ash

JULY 17, 2001

Loneliness may endeavor
to invade the heart.
Yet a happy countenance,
disciplined diligence, and joy
break the advancing line.

JULY 30, 2001

- In attempting to spark creativity, I feel quite helpless. Maybe the key is not to think so much. Yet what if those hours of slide-show memories eventually find their way into a cohesive montage?

- What of love? A smile, a glance, a hidden stare? Love is careful observation of one's true nature.

- Where is the heart? Does it lie within the mind? Is it a matter of conquering the will?

- Emotions show much more than we try to hide.

- One of life's greatest gifts is unfaltering trust. A shared, unspoken understanding into which one can enter without fear of crumbling. Trust planted in fertile soil will blossom into lifelong friendship and mutual understanding. Planted in clay, it will bring only heartache, fear, and decay.

- Love thrives on the principle of trust. Why harm your fellow man?

ANXIETY
by Olivia Ash

100% at 100% drains,
Leeching life energy.
Disappointment cuts like a knife through soft tissue.
My soul yearns for space, peace, and rest.

LIGHT
by Olivia Ash

When time wears upon you
And anxiety consumes vibrant life,
Turn your eye above,
From whence comes your inner light.

AUGUST 6, 2001

Utter frustration. Time permeated by yelling, bickering, and hate becomes a broken record. My ears numb to the sound. It's been years and I have no more tears.

AUGUST 9, 2002

Finally, no work. 71 degrees, slight breeze from the left, warm and sunny. Undisturbed droplets of water hover on the grass, awaiting my steps. Alone and thinking, the trees speak to me of rest, relaxation, and challenge. A challenge to play, to push the limits, and to revel in the beauty and calm of this moment.

Angry, bitter, and frustrated, tears descend. My glass house of safety is cracking. Will it work out? How can I continue? Yet among fractured fears and doubts, peace slips in. She glides, ever quiet and calm. Calming, Soothing, Healing.

KEEP GOING
Evansville, Indiana

MAY 2003

By the time undergraduate graduation arrived, I had entered an "arrangement" with chronic pain, thanks to summers of negotiations via surgery and journaling. I wrote poetry to express what I could (and could not) see and feel. I walked the paces of post-operative healing and physical therapy, preparing for another season of competition. I left campus with a bachelor's degree, a metal plate, six screws, and multiple joint surgeries to my credit. I never knew which pain would resurface, and so I kept going. That was the best option.

SOMETHING'S MISSING

Downtown Indianapolis, Indiana

DECEMBER 25, 2004

It's supposed to be a joyous occasion, right? Yet the eerie silence whispered words of warning to my heart as I accepted the folded paper from his hand. There was little verbal expression of his love. Can't he share how he feels?

I recall the scene with clarity as crisp as the cold winter air of that evening. I was facing north, wearing a blue woolen coat. He was on bended knee wearing khakis, oblivious to the fresh dusting of snow on the concrete. The butterfly enclosure to the west was illuminated, yet I noted only the two of us that still night. So still. So serene. So silent.

I did not expect to read the night he proposed. I see his faint script in memory, and sadness yawns. I attempted to untangle the dissonance between his taciturn communication and my naïve expectation of a "knight in shining armor." I could barely read the charcoal scrawls in the dim light. I swiftly read his proposal as the weight of anticipation within the winter breeze intensified.

I accepted, of course, because I loved him. Relief washed over me, and I hoped that in living together, we would grow in intimacy. Yet I admit I cannot recall whether he ever spoke the words, "Will you marry me?"

THE ABSENCE OF PRESENCE

A restaurant, Westfield, Indiana

JULY 30, 2005

"Look, Mommy! It's a princess." I barely glimpsed the girl's face as she reached her hand towards me. I recall her voice (and the venue's taupe walls) with poignancy. Less than two hours before, we vowed to love one another till death parted us. Weddings are chaos, even if small and funded by meager graduate student earnings. Yet even in chaos, I couldn't shake the memory of his demeanor at the altar, standing within inches of my face. He appeared petrified.

Tears poured from my eyes as I spoke, allowing the meaning of each vow to land, one by one, like molten metal into the cast of my heart. I've been accused of being "too serious." I prefer the word "intense." It was an intense moment; I was committing body and property to a man with whom I'd never cohabitated, let alone shared a bed.

How hopeful I was when the little girl spoke those words! The contrast between the authentic, joyful eruption from her heart with his stoic, taciturn responses resounded like a gong trapped in my chest. She could see that I was pretty—that I was enough. She thought I was a prize worth cherishing. And yet, in the muffled conversation of wedding guests, I don't recall the presence of my shiny new husband basking in the bliss of unity. I see only visions of laughing with friends and strangers.

ANSWERS
South Bend, Indiana

MAY 5, 2007

My spirit was as gray as the skies staring back at me as I drove north. Once again, I was searching for answers. I knew deep within something was wrong with my body. The shadows of headache, exhaustion, and ceaseless pain followed me, especially on cloudy days. I couldn't figure out why, and that fueled annoyance. I wanted to move, to play, and to feel happy. The dichotomy between balancing my desire for freedom with chronic pain management from unknown sources drained my life energy.

"We won't 'diagnose' you with a Chiari Malformation, as imaging shows your brain is 'on the line,' but you'll experience symptoms." The specialist stated this with the nonchalance of a speaker calling out numbers at Saturday night bingo. My cerebellum was "slumping" into the space reserved for my brainstem, creating pressure, and causing pain, intermittent nausea, and dizziness. It was not an optimal diagnosis, but it did not require surgery.

A Chiari Malformation may occur with my diagnosis of Hypermobile Ehlers-Danlos Syndrome (hEDS), a heritable connective tissue disorder characterized by collagen degeneration, joint hypermobility and instability, and chronic pain. The collagen within my body is deteriorating like a rubber band forgotten in the junk drawer. Weak collagen within my body fails over time, tearing little by little, and sometimes—with enough force—tears a lot. Therefore, popping, grinding, and pain greet me each morning to remind me of my limitations.

Doctors advised me I could expect a lifetime of ever-weakening body systems because collagen is king. It's a structural protein throughout the body, responsible for strength and integrity. It's a flexible web supporting most tissues. I inherited a faulty web, meaning all my systems are affected by the genetic abnormality. It requires lifetime maintenance and lifestyle adjustments.

Despite this diagnosis, as I grappled with facing a lifetime of pain management, relief arrived. A spring of hope bubbled; I could do something with facts. I had endured eight orthopedic surgeries and their recovery in my twenty-six years. I played four years of collegiate athletics. My body was tired, and the solitary internal struggle with relentless pain fed loneliness—with whom could I explain the constancy of this weariness and these aches? Who would understand?

The unknown is a scary place. We spend our waking hours seeking the fleeting zephyr of control: planning our days, weeks, months, and lives—all before we have lived them. Yet we need to feel control, a sense of autonomy, over our bodies. Though the specialist recommended I not bear children and begin taking an antidepressant, peace settled. I was exhausted and saddened by this news, but because I could act through learning and application, levity alighted my outlook.

I would turn this news into lemonade. Using strength of mind to balance bodily weakness, I would learn how to manage chronic pain by listening to it and my body. Listen. Learn. Try. Repeat. Trying makes all the difference.

PLAN B
Indianapolis, Indiana

We used protection, but there was a chance.

I didn't want to take it; deep within, it felt unnatural. I know we discussed reasons for not having children: My body could not handle the physical stress, and he didn't want kids. I didn't think I'd be a successful mother. I felt broken and unworthy because my body ached, and I had not yet healed from traumas.

The decision impatiently paced on the threshold of my mind.

I know we said "No" to children, but what if?

Perhaps I can do it—we can do it—we can raise a child.

I did not voice it, but my mind spoke in resistance: *I don't want to do this. I don't want to do this alone. Aren't we a team?*

Yet, I did it. I drove to the pharmacy, alone. I shamefully requested it, alone. And I sat on the side of my bed, staring at the white pill, alone. My body did not want to abort the possibility of a new life. I knew that once ingested, there was no going back.

I swallowed the white circle of certainty, thwarting any possibility.

Facing the western sun, I felt sick—heartsick. Yet it was non-negotiable. I married him; we had discussed it. He adamantly voiced his stance. He did not want to be a father; he once quipped he could barely "take care of himself." My mind reflected on this statement, and I burned within.

If he doesn't think he can take care of himself, what about our marriage? Shell-shocked from soul to sole, I still nurtured unconscious hope. I wanted to be held by him, to feel comfort, and to nurture possibility. I don't recall that need met. Anger grew, and parallel to it—sadness. The distance between our perspectives increased. And in this space, loneliness thrived. The gap between us shifted to reveal a valley. The bond between me, myself, and I cracked; my soul slowly seeped into the chasm below.

HISTORY REPEATS ITSELF
Indianapolis, Indiana

FEBRUARY 2009

I unconsciously adopted her coping mechanism, knowing deep within it brought me breadcrumbs of sustenance. Yet, like an addiction, it also brought momentary relief, a high within the seemingly solution-less maze of relational despair. I let them bleach my long, virgin hair—multiple times—then chop it off into an asymmetric helmet. As my hair turned from Peep yellow to the coolest of platinum, my scalp's skin seared like ham in a frying pan. They used scissors, razors, and purple dye. I cried within at my desperate decision as the bleach burned.

Apparently, its European flair gave "cool, edgy" vibes, reminiscent of punk-grunge aesthetics. Yet I festered within. I had given birth to what I absorbed a decade before, except this time I was the one shorn. Because it was "modeling," I felt justified in seeking a new look whenever loneliness threatened to flood the boundaries of my heart.

He detested it, and very likely me. That was my verdict, given the look on his face and the literal distance he placed between us when I walked in the door smelling like a patched-up salon accident. My attempts to be "fresh," "sexy," and "exciting" garnered further distance and weaker communication instead of curiosity and support. He did not touch me for days. How did I respond?

I repeated this cycle of stylish self-harm for six years, hoping the next iteration of me would be acceptable. I explained it away, "It's only hair, it will grow back." I wove this excuse into my love of art and fashion; it filled my own broken cup. I grasped at the mirage of affirmation as loneliness took root in my soul.

ALONE ON A LONELY ROAD

Indianapolis, Indiana

2009

It ached too badly to ignore. He had to work the next morning, so I drove alone. The only place open that late was the Urgent Care off Hazel Dell Road. It was a painful twenty-minute drive. Exhausted from a recent surgery, my back throbbed. The night was clear, the sky black. I hunched over the steering wheel like Cruella De Vil as she tore through the countryside in her Panther, hell-bent on securing her precious puppies.

They found blood in my urine. An angry kidney infection flared after the latest surgery to move the ulnar nerve in my right arm so I could regain feeling in two fingers. Because I didn't exhibit classic symptoms of a urinary tract infection, the infection spread until I could barely tolerate abdominal movement.

Thankfully, antibiotics and rest were the solution—at least for my body. The pain within did not subside with rest. I survived another surgery and its side effects mostly alone. He didn't take me to the hospital the morning of surgery. He wasn't emotionally engaged when I craved affection and my back ached. And he didn't assist me—let alone sit beside me— as I drove myself towards a solution. He had a routine, and I failed to speak up for my needs.

LONELINESS: 101

Loneliness is perception. Loneliness is not social isolation. It is not solitude. It is perceived isolation. In 2018, 54% of Americans reported feeling "lonely," with 46% rating themselves as "sometimes or always feeling lonely."[11] In 2020, the rate of loneliness in the U.S. jumped to 61%,[12] and returned to approximately 50% in 2021.[13] Only 39% of American adults reported feeling "very connected" to others.[14]

According to the U.S. Surgeon General's 2023 Advisory, loneliness is "a subjective distressing experience that results from perceived isolation or inadequate meaningful connections, where inadequate refers to the discrepancy or unmet need between an individual's preferred and actual experience."[15] Loneliness is an aversive, distressing emotion and response to a mental state. It is subjective and refers to a deficiency in a person's social relationships in terms of type, quality, or quantity relative to a perceived need.

Loneliness is not isolation. Loneliness is a unique-to-you emotion that science cannot pin down. It is a *quali*tative measure, not *quan*titative.

Think *quality*, not *quantity*. It's not a measure of *how many*; it's a measure of *what it's like*. We create words, scales, and charts to observe behaviors driven by loneliness, but we cannot measure it like isolation. We can measure the number of social contacts (i.e., persons you encounter) in your life. However, loneliness and isolation are tethered—meaning one affects the other by degrees, and observing this interplay permits us to explore strategies to manage each.

Loneliness is a subjective experience, meaning it's your *felt sense* of lacking. It's your perception of what you have compared to what you want, filtered through your personality, experiences, and how you interpret your life—including everything in (and lacking from) it. Loneliness is founded on a simple relationship between two factors: what you have and need, measured against what you desire. The degree of difference between these is the intensity of loneliness. It's the space between. And that gap hurts—you feel the absence of desired meaning.

When we feel lonely, it's as though we are the only one making mistakes. This, in turn, magnifies the shame, guilt, or inadequacy felt.[16] It is possible to feel lonely at a concert and satisfied in solitude. Your heart may burst with gratitude at a coffee date with a friend yet shrivel in a sea of social connections. You may be married for years, yet feel the icy pang of loneliness day in and out. Or you may be single and sassy, sucking the marrow from life and throwing caution (and relationships) to the wind while you solo climb Devils Tower. You are unique; your experience of "without" is unique to you.

LONELINESS   V.   ISOLATION

↓

Lack of
companionship
or a useful
role at home,
society, or
In your job.

↓

Separation
from social
or familiar
contact,
community,
or access
to services.

↘   ↙

Your PERCEPTION of missing these
compared to your DESIRE is
LONELINESS

Liv Ash

Loneliness is multi-faceted; how I process it looks different from how others process it. This is the subjective nature of the emotion. Our personalities, upbringing, trauma, and well-being affect our expressions and levels of loneliness. Research divides the emotion into two main types—emotional and social loneliness. Anxiety is common to both. Emotional loneliness feels distressing and may mimic feeling abandoned because we need intimate relationships. Social loneliness makes concentration tough and is expressed as boredom and aimlessness. It may feel like being "left out."

Loneliness hurts—literally and metaphysically—our bodies and psyches. We are not meant to live in a state of chronic loneliness. Research indicates increasing loneliness weakens our physical health. The lonelier we become, the more ill we become, in body and soul. Loneliness is a painful void few admit to feeling, let alone discussing. I believe loneliness exists as an alarm, calling us to act to alleviate it.

Research confirms we are social creatures, and desire to be in supportive relationships. Without them, we wilt; we withdraw; we lessen. I believe the only way to lessen loneliness is to *Ask & Act,*[17] to learn what we want and need. Gradual alignment of our desires with actions lessens lonely feelings. Feeling lonely drives us to seek well-being behaviors such as talk therapy and mindfulness, and to practice inclusion by seeking supportive social circles. Feeling lonely and feeling included are opposing forces.[18] Therefore, a powerful tool to manage loneliness is the concept of inclusion. We must learn our way out of loneliness, and that may be a difficult lesson to learn.

LONELINESS FEELS LIKE

→ Isolation

→ Aimelessness

→ Boredom

→ Being left out

→ Fear

→ Emptiness

→ Being without

→ Discomfort

→ Something is missing

LivAsh

4 MAIN CONTRIBUTORS TO LONELINESS

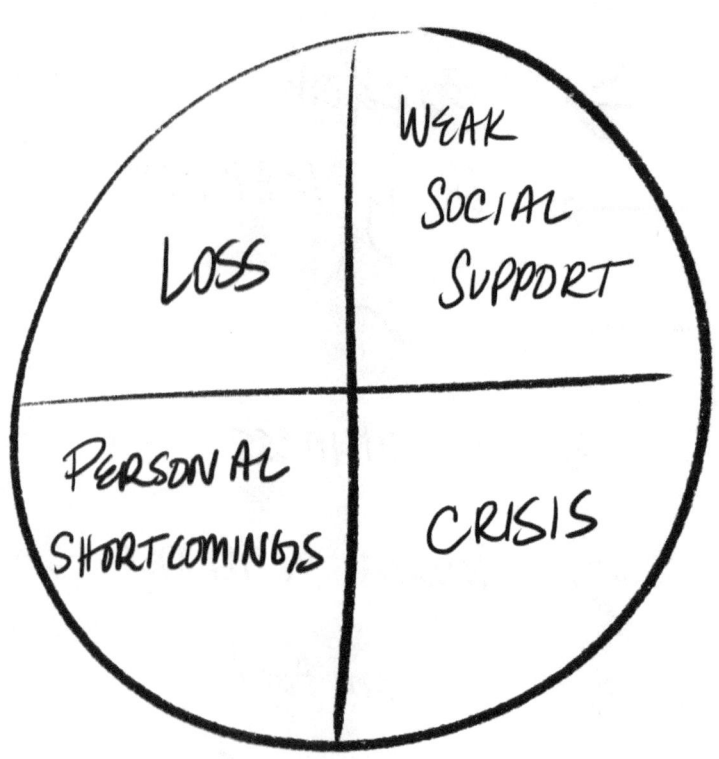

LOSS

WEAK SOCIAL SUPPORT

PERSONAL SHORTCOMINGS

CRISIS

Liv Ash

CONTRIBUTORS TO LONELINESS

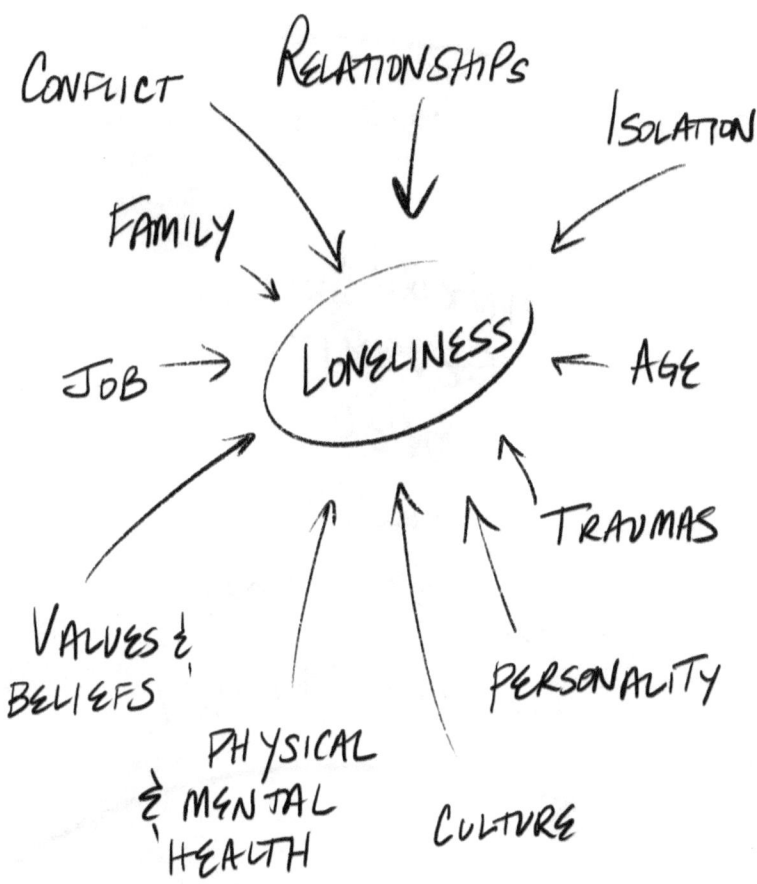

CONFLICT

RELATIONSHIPS

ISOLATION

FAMILY

JOB

LONELINESS

AGE

TRAUMAS

VALUES &
BELIEFS

PERSONALITY

PHYSICAL
& MENTAL
HEALTH

CULTURE

Liv Ash

SOCIAL CONDITIONS AFFECTING LONELINESS

INEQUALITY
SEVERITY
POVERTY
SCARCITY
COMPETITION
INDIVIDUALISM

Livtsh

WHO IS LONELY?
(STATISTICS)

Age — <25
⟩ 65

Sex — males & females report ≈ levels

Gender — higher levels in LGBTQ community

Partnership — higher levels for single, divorced, & widowed

Liv Ash

Who is Lonely?
(Statistics)

Adolescence – teens struggle to build self-esteem & need healthy friendships.

Friendship – Quality friends are essential to managing loneliness.

Liv Ash

WHY SO LONELY?
(STATISTICS)

Personality

Genetics & emotional expression affect loneliness and resiliency. Lonelier people are more: shy, anxious, hostile, socially awkward, and have lower self-esteem.

Listen

The Lonely Personality

BEHAVIORS

- TALKED MORE ABOUT SELF.

- CRITICIZED OTHERS.

- PERCEIVED SELF NEGATIVELY.

- LACKED EMPATY.

- AVOIDED INTIMACY.

Livtsh

TABLE A – 10 TYPES OF LONELINESS & THEIR CHARACTERISTICS

10 TYPES OF LONELINESS[19]	
Cosmic	The feeling or premonition that not only are beings unconnected, but that there is no transcendent person or personal power. Characterized by a sense of being alone in the universe, void of any ultimate, personalized meaning, and feeling that evil is metaphysically and objectively real.
Cultural	Persons and groups of persons who deem themselves excluded, left out, overlooked, unconnected to, or disconnected from the mainstream. Characterized by a lack of cohesion and identity that resembles alienation but is not the same. May be felt by minorities and certain age and gender groups. Persons exhibit negative emotions and thoughts towards oneself and others. Caused by and causing low self-worth.
Emotional	The essence of this type of loneliness is a lack of passion that connects a person to meaning in life. If absent, a person is either lonely or bored or both. *Eros* loneliness is a lack of shared intimacies (erotic, romantic, sexual, or genital). A deficiency of intimacy and failure at sharing oneself produces a feeling of self-depreciation. If pervasive, there may exist a "deep and abiding loneliness" felt as anguished self-failure.

Epistemological	A mental state encompassing negative attitudes towards physical aloneness. Characterized by a lack of desired relationships and recognizing individuality. Intimacy as self-disclosure is both sought and resisted. One feels their presence goes unnoticed and their absence isn't missed. This may be a result of choosing not to know or to be known; believing others do not wish to invest emotional energy in them; or believing their singularity is unacceptable, unappealing, or misunderstood. This may be due to defective communication, an inability or unwillingness to be attuned to verbal and non-verbal messages, or from incompetence in social skills. Emotions and emotional states include self-worthlessness, anxiety, frustration, shame, anger, depressiveness, sorrow, and fear. A lack of self-worth leads to poor social composure, leading to insufficient assertiveness and risk taking. This may lead to private and public self-consciousness and shyness (which may negatively reinforce each other). Persons exhibit inappropriate and abnormal tendencies in self-disclosure, thereby revealing too much or too little. There's a tendency to be highly self-focused, self-absorbed, make too many self-statements, and ask fewer questions of their partners. Persons change topics more frequently and show less interest in others' statements and are remiss in both social and solitary skills. Persons experience an inability to communicate feelings. For schizophrenics, profound loneliness causes noncommunication broken only by auditory delusions.

Ethical	Philosophically, loneliness is inherent in freedom, choice, responsibility, and value formation. Loneliness and solitude are essential conditions and catalysts for achieving moral superiority, i.e., being "lonely-at-the-top."
Existential	The loneliness of the human experience and recognition of an essential loneliness that persists throughout life. Seen in and increased by specific situations, lifestyles, occupations, and societal factors.
Intrapersonal	A feeling of division or divisibility of one's self-identity. Persons may have "parents who are perceived as remote and untrustworthy" instead of being "warm, close, and helpful," and come from families who furnish less "emotional nurturance, guidance, or support," and are therefore a product of "cold, violent, undisciplined, and irrational" home environments.
Metaphysical	The most comprehensive and pervasive type of loneliness. Considered a "master mood" and one's "perception of reality." Life may feel "out of place" and "without connection and continuity."

Social	*Friendship* loneliness is a lack of intimate sharing (friendship, friendliness, companionship, social networks, and shared common experiences). The essence of this type of loneliness is a lack of passion that connects a person to meaning in life. If absent, a person is either lonely or bored or both.
	Intimacy is the most personal aspect of subjectivity, i.e., "meaning," in its spiritual, mental, and physical dimensions. Intimacy liberates a person from subjective narcissism and selfishness. It concerns the innermost self and the surrender of it. Intimacy involves the freedom and selectivity of when and with whom to share it. When it grows, one grows empowered in harmony with others, promoting integrity and identity.

WHY SO LONELY?
(STATS)

Time Online

Spending more time online increased isolation in relationships, emotional disconnection, anxiety, and mental fatigue.

Liv Ash

SURVEY: PAINTING THE LANDSCAPE OF LONELINESS	
PARTICIPANT SUBMISSION	
Age Range	30 – 39
Race & Ethnicity & Sex	Mixed race; White and Hispanic female
Education Stats	Some college; no degree
Employment Stats	Employed, full time
Current Level of Loneliness	Low/Moderate

Please describe a time in your life when you felt lonely.

I work in ministry in a church. I'm surrounded by people all the time. When things politically were at an all-time high a couple of years ago, friends who I thought were family started to leave the ministry. There was so much tension in the world. I felt very lonely and sad. There were days when my husband would tell me to get up and out of bed. There were days when all I could do was sit and watch TV. I'm surrounded by people and have a very wonderful family and work family, but that season was the most isolated and lonely I've ever felt in my life. I was grieving the loss of people who were like family, and it hurt deeply. My loneliness was high.

SURVEY: PAINTING THE LANDSCAPE OF LONELINESS	
PARTICIPANT SUBMISSION	
Age Range	30 – 39
Race & Ethnicity & Sex	White female
Education Stats	Bachelor's degree
Employment Stats	Employed, full-time remote
Current Level of Loneliness	Moderate

Please describe a time in your life when you felt lonely.

When my boyfriend and I broke up after a few years together, my best friend moved to a different place. It felt lonely in my 3D world despite having many other friends and support I was in touch with remotely. I don't mind being alone, but knowing I had lost my closest people felt very lonely. Also, being at the age where most friends are married or have kids added to the loneliness and sadness. My loneliness felt high for a few months; now it feels moderate.

SURVEY: PAINTING THE LANDSCAPE OF LONELINESS	
PARTICIPANT SUBMISSION	
Age Range	30 – 39
Race & Ethnicity & Sex	White female
Education Stats	Associate's degree
Employment Stats	Employed, part-time, remote
Current Level of Loneliness	Moderate/High

Please describe a time in your life when you felt lonely.

My husband is a neurodivergent introvert, and I struggle to connect with him sometimes and express how I feel. I am more extroverted and highly empathetic, and he can sometimes dismiss me as "too emotional." We had a community in the church, but after the pandemic we both left the church, and all we really have is each other.

We love each other, but building new community often leaves me feeling alone, even in a room full of people. In addition to the pandemic, we are new parents and had our baby during the pandemic alone and without help, support, or advice. The last three years have been the loneliest time I have ever experienced.

SURVEY: PAINTING THE LANDSCAPE OF LONELINESS	
PARTICIPANT SUBMISSION	
Age Range	30 – 39
Race & Ethnicity & Sex	White female
Education Stats	Bachelor's degree
Employment Stats	Not employed, not looking for work
Current Level of Loneliness	Low/Moderate
Please describe a time in your life when you felt lonely.	
Relocating. Kids were in school. Husband was working. Left me to be alone a lot. Only connected through phone and social media.	

SURVEY: PAINTING THE LANDSCAPE OF LONELINESS	
PARTICIPANT SUBMISSION	
Age Range	40 – 49
Race & Ethnicity & Sex	White female
Education Stats	Bachelor's degree
Employment Stats	Employed, working remotely
Current Level of Loneliness	Moderate/High

Please describe a time in your life when you felt lonely.

I started a new job at a small company in a newly created position. My manager spent a couple hours showing me around the office, introducing me to 50 people, and providing a brief background. After that initial meet and greet, she left for a week-long trip.

I was embarrassed. I didn't remember anyone's names from the introductions. She told me one person I could ask questions of, but he seemed a bit stand-offish. I was left with an overwhelming project to tackle and no friendly faces. My role was new, so there was no documentation or previous work to reference. I felt lonely, unwelcome, and unsure of what to do next. I would rate my loneliness as high.

SURVEY: PAINTING THE LANDSCAPE OF LONELINESS	
PARTICIPANT SUBMISSION	
Age Range	40 – 49
Race & Ethnicity & Sex	Mixed race female
Education Stats	Bachelor's degree
Employment Stats	Stay-at-home mom
Current Level of Loneliness	Moderate
Please describe a time in your life when you felt lonely.	
Motherhood and raising a young family mostly alone feels lonely.	

SURVEY: PAINTING THE LANDSCAPE OF LONELINESS	
PARTICIPANT SUBMISSION	
Age Range	40 – 49
Race & Ethnicity & Sex	White female
Education Stats	Graduate degree
Employment Stats	Self-employed mom
Current Level of Loneliness	Low/Moderate

Please describe a time in your life when you felt lonely.

In my twenties I moved abroad by myself for adventure and work. I knew no one in the cities I lived in, and it was extremely difficult to forge new relationships. Language was one of the main barriers. Sometimes there was merely being "alone" and having quiet, peace, and solitude, enjoying the time to do what I wanted, when I wanted.

Then, a lot of the time there was "loneliness" with no one to talk to when needing or wanting to talk—whether for camaraderie or something deeper. There was no one to enjoy the surroundings or good weather with. No one to watch a TV show and then dissect together. There was a sense of boredom, of just wasting time. I questioned, "What am I doing? Why am I here? Where am I going?"

There was also a deep, deep homesickness for friends, family, and places that I knew and loved. A deep longing to be around people who knew and understood me on a cultural and personal level. My loneliness at these times was extremely high.

SURVEY: PAINTING THE LANDSCAPE OF LONELINESS	
PARTICIPANT SUBMISSION	
Age Range	30 – 39
Race & Ethnicity & Sex	White male
Education Stats	Some college; no degree
Employment Stats	Employed, full-time
Current Level of Loneliness	Moderate
Please describe a time in your life when you felt lonely.	
After a breakup. The feeling of not having someone I can go to at any time.	

SURVEY: PAINTING THE LANDSCAPE OF LONELINESS	
PARTICIPANT SUBMISSION	
Age Range	40 – 49
Race & Ethnicity & Sex	Mixed race; Scotch Irish American male
Education Stats	Bachelor's degree
Employment Stats	Employed, remote
Current Level of Loneliness	High
Please describe a time in your life when you felt lonely.	

My partner moved out of the state with our kids. I had about five weeks where I lived in a huge house by myself, walking past empty rooms that once held children and a master bedroom that held a marriage. I was 700 miles from most of my network. This was the height of loneliness.

SURVEY: PAINTING THE LANDSCAPE OF LONELINESS	
PARTICIPANT SUBMISSION	
Age Range	60+
Race & Ethnicity & Sex	White male
Education Stats	Graduate degree
Employment Stats	Employed, part-time remote work
Current Level of Loneliness	Low
Please describe a time in your life when you felt lonely.	
My teens.	

SURVEY: PAINTING THE LANDSCAPE OF LONELINESS	
PARTICIPANT SUBMISSION	
Age Range	60+
Race & Ethnicity & Sex	White male
Education Stats	Some college; no degree
Employment Stats	Retired
Current Level of Loneliness	High

Please describe a time in your life when you felt lonely.

Three months ago, my youngest son and I parted ways. We haven't communicated in three months. After all we do for our children, this is how we get paid back. I've been a single parent for over fifteen years. I am old school; I held all my children to a high level, maybe too high for all of them. Same goes with close friends—always had a high expectation for all, and now hardly interact with most of them. I would rate my loneliness as high.

Economic Impact of Loneliness

$960 Billion

⬇

Annual Cost To Treat:

⬇

→ Depression

→ Suicide

→ Substance Misuse

⬇

Loneliness is a <u>Major</u>
Cause of each

<u>Liv Ash</u>

SURVEY: PAINTING THE LANDSCAPE OF LONELINESS	
PARTICIPANT SUBMISSION	
Age Range	30 – 39
Race & Ethnicity & Sex	White female
Education Stats	Doctorate degree
Employment Stats	Employed, full-time remote
Current Level of Loneliness	Low

Please describe a time in your life when you felt lonely.

In the fall of 2021, I had experienced four failed bar exams and had recently decided to come off hormonal contraceptives. I was working in the legal profession, barely able to pay my bills, and I was cleaning Airbnb's on Sundays for 8–10 hours. I had never felt so alone and like a failure. My hormones were unstable from stopping hormonal contraceptives, and I had a law school degree but was barely making ends meet.

I felt like no one was able to relate or understand how I was feeling or what I'd gone through. I felt like there was no light at the end of the tunnel. I felt like a complete failure and that it was all for nothing. I felt like nothing, and that no one and nothing could help me. I would sit on the couch with a knife to my throat and my wrist to see what it felt like. I started thinking through the best ways to unalive myself. I was 32 years old at the time. My loneliness at that time was high. Very high. And very scary.

WHY SO LONELY?
(STATS)

Occupation — lonely
workers feel less
job satisfaction,
switch jobs more often,
and feel less support.
In 2018, lawyers
and doctors rated
the loneliest of
American workers.

Liv Ash

SURVEY: PAINTING THE LANDSCAPE OF LONELINESS	
PARTICIPANT SUBMISSION	
Age Range	40 – 49
Race & Ethnicity & Sex	White, Mexican female
Education Stats	Doctorate degree
Employment Stats	Employed, full-time hybrid
Current Level of Loneliness	Moderate

Please describe a time in your life when you felt lonely.

When searching for a job or any financial hardship, loneliness is high.

Author's Note: This participant submitted a short essay on her experience with loneliness as a lawyer and First-Generation Person (FGP). In a 2018 survey of American workers, lawyers rated the loneliest.[20] Factors affecting rates of loneliness include the following: loss, crisis, occupation, level of education, personal shortcomings, traumas, social support, divorce, living alone, personality type, specific cultural experiences, and being a member of a minority group.

I have never been in a room where I have felt like an imposter, and I have been in some amazing rooms with successful, brilliant people. There were times in those rooms that my role was learner, paralegal, HR generalist, manager, and most lately, attorney. I never felt as though I did not deserve to sit at the table; however, as both a first-generation student and graduate, I have felt like an outlier or "other." Employers and colleagues did not know what to do with me until they interacted with me because my path does not resemble either a "traditional" career or educational path.

It is a lonely battle to try to get into the right rooms. A First-Generation Person is a student or graduate who does not have at least one parent or guardian with a Bachelor's degree or higher. They face certain challenges in the practice of law. I was taught, like other FGPs, to get an education, be the hardest worker in the room, and pursue perfection, and in turn, rooms where decisions are made will open. This is not the case.

The pursuit of perfection combined with tremendous work responsibilities and part-time law school nearly broke me. My family could not understand what I was going through, nor could my friends or work colleagues. I was blessed with camaraderie from my law school cohorts, but explaining to people who have always seen you thrive, while working hard and maintaining family obligations, was impossible. I had never been through an experience where my family was unable to emotionally support me, let alone an experience that lasted four years. It was entirely outside the scope of what they knew; I felt entirely on my own.

Law schools will tell you that law school should be your top priority, and it should be—unless you have financial responsibilities like families, mortgages, and a desire not to graduate with $118,000 in school debt. I couldn't even identify or admit to myself that I had feelings of loneliness. Compared to the problems my parents faced raising, feeding, and clothing four children, loneliness as a problem seemed absurd. I felt that I should be "tougher" or "grittier" than to feel "down" and lonely.

However, once I began trying to understand what I was experiencing (the first-generation challenges cited in multiple studies), I began not to feel alone, and that felt good. It hit me one day how alone I felt when

I told my parents (who couldn't understand) about job interviews and how "traditional" lawyers looked down on me because I didn't take the "traditional" path. I had managed teams of people and a multi-million-dollar benefit plan. I served as a criminal law paralegal. Yet in interviews among attorneys, multiple lawyers asked me, "How do you expect to get a job as a lawyer without interning or clerking?" In those moments, I had not felt so alone since childhood.

According to the National Association of Law Placement, FGPs are worse off in the job market after graduation compared to peers who have at least one parent or guardian with a law degree. In the annual research report, "Jobs & JDs, Employment and Salaries of New Graduates, Class of 2020," a survey indicated the employment rate was nearly 93% for those who had at least one parent holding a J.D. degree, and 88% for FGPs. Meanwhile, the rate of employment for FGPs in bar-passage-required jobs was more than 11 percentage points lower than peers at 73%.

My mother still tells me, "Work speaks for itself. You do not need a network. People will hear of the quality of your work, and you will get the work." This has not been my experience. My network of lawyers is the most valued asset I possess. Because of this community of lawyers, I get legal work, my name is mentioned in rooms where I'm not present, and they serve as my biggest cheerleaders on social media, a critical element of my business.

How did I finally recognize and accept that I was "lonely"? When I started researching the challenges of other FGPs and meeting face-to-face with people like me, I felt a sense of camaraderie, and therefore, less alone. I learned that loneliness, for me, is a word that not only encompasses the lack of social engagement or feelings of belonging but also means hopelessness.

However, when people cheer you on, provide you fresh ideas, and provide support (i.e., you can rest with them), there is hope that what you are trying to achieve is possible. Once I began connecting with other lawyers from similar backgrounds, I learned that—even as adults—they are still plagued by internal expectations of perfectionism. The burden of perfectionism created a need to consistently over-prepare and contributed to them earning an education that has yet to provide a return on investment.

Once I began to identify this tendency within me, I was able to thoughtfully identify what was required of myself for a certain project (i.e., how much preparation should rationally be done, or what level of education was necessary, etc.). This has allowed me to invest time and resources where appropriate. As far as "perfect"? There is no such thing. Work Product is "due," not "done." If the pursuit of perfectionism causes assignments to be late at the cost of unnecessary resources, perfectionism can be debilitating.

For me, building a community forced me to be vulnerable. For a lifetime I tried to hide who I was; in turn, vulnerability felt excruciating. I must tell my story with the hope that others will share their stories as well. Some of my biggest cheerleaders do not share my background. But because they understand certain challenges and my reluctance to ask for help, they assist and push me in ways I could not have imagined. To build my community, I was forced to look inward; being vulnerable has made all the difference to my business and my mental health.

WHY SO LONELY?
(STATISTICS)

Culture - our
attitudes and
beliefs
about acceptable
emotional behaviors
affect how we
build friends,
interact, and
perceive loneliness.

Liv Ash

SURVEY: PAINTING THE LANDSCAPE OF LONELINESS	
PARTICIPANT SUBMISSION – VAL'S STORY	
Age	64
Race & Ethnicity & Sex	White, Bulgarian female
Education Stats	Bachelor's degree
Employment Stats	Employed; full-time stylist
Current Level of Loneliness	Low

Author's Note: Val requested an in-person interview, as she is not a native English speaker. She requested to share her story via conversation instead of completing the online survey. Val speaks multiple languages, and upon moving to the United States, taught herself English. With the support of a Bulgarian community in Philadelphia, she assimilated well, even as her marriage deteriorated. When she moved her family to Chicago, loneliness grew. Isolated and without community support, negativity in her marriage exponentially increased her lonely feelings.

Our interview occurred in Southwest Florida on July 22, 2023— the date of her 45th wedding anniversary. Though married, she lives separately from her husband. A 75-year Harvard study indicated that the quality of our relationships is the number one predictor of our quality of life.[21] This applies to relationships of all types: friendships, work colleagues, family dynamics, and, most impactful, our intimate relationships. When any of these relationships is unhealthy or not fulfilling desired needs, we feel loneliness and learn to cope. How we cope affects our well-being.

We manage loneliness through practicing mindfulness; speaking with trusted persons such as friends or a licensed therapist (i.e., talk therapy); and being in community with those who have shared experiences or with whom we share interests (i.e., inclusion). With permission, I have edited our interview for concision and clarity, while honoring the original syntax. Val requested I use her first name. Her voice is in italicized font; bracketed words are added for clarity. This is Val's story of how she's learned to manage loneliness.

Author: Please describe a time in your life when you felt lonely. Explain how you felt and describe the context. This may include your emotions, the place, the people, and the events. Please rate your loneliness at the time.

Val: After we moved from Pennsylvania to Illinois to be close to my daughter and the grandkids, that's when I started to feel lonely. Because my husband is a very jealous person.

Author's Note: Val and I chatted for a few minutes when I realized I was missing pieces of her story that would help my understanding, describe her level of loneliness, and illustrate how it developed. Val started at the beginning.

Val: I came to the United States because of his mother. She was an even worse control freak [than her husband]. His father was a Hydro engineer, drilling for water. Back then, Bulgaria was a communist country. My father-in-law built a big house for his wife and kids. In

Europe, it's called a family house. We [Val and her husband] started living there after our marriage with his parents and his sister.

My father-in-law was a great man. He never once mentioned what he did for us—not even once. But there was my mother-in-law: every moment she would tell me that, thanks to them, we [Val and her husband] had a house. Thanks to them, we had a car. He bought everything for us.

I opened my first salon. My salon was part of the house; we lived on the third level. I worked only by appointments, and [back then] people were not used to that. I was booked a few weeks ahead. I was very famous. People in the capital knew me. College guys would go to the capital for university but come back to me to get their hair done. I was driving her crazy because her kids were not famous, I was. She [complained about my business]. I was raised not to talk back. But one day, I said to my mother-in-law, "Listen, they [customers] need to know when I'm off. I'm not working 24/7."

She made everything a big deal; that's the reason I decided to move my family out of the country, away from her. I never felt like I was a married person. She was always between us. This was the custom in my country many years ago. I felt like a little child. More specifically, I felt like a disabled little child. I decided to prove that I could do more than she thought I could. I was very young when I had my daughter; I was 19. I did everything that my inner voice and my senses told me.

When I arrived [in the United States], I started cleaning houses; you have to make a living somehow, and I'm not ashamed to do anything. My daughter was eighteen years old [when they arrived] and my son younger. We lived fifteen years in Philadelphia. I started learning English after my first hair show in Paris [when she lived in Bulgaria].

I learned English two years before [we moved], but it wasn't enough. I needed to learn it for my business.

I came to a different planet; a different lifestyle in the States than what I knew. I was not lonely when I arrived because I was so busy and I was building my new life, so I had to be patient. I spent five years cleaning and learning a language 24/7. I didn't feel lonely back then. I met many Bulgarians in Philadelphia. I was busy; I didn't have time to be lonely.

Loneliness came after we moved to Illinois. [We moved because my daughter left.] We told her, "Go where you want, we will pay your tuition. We need you to finish college." Chicago has an interior design school (and the biggest Bulgarian community). She met her husband, married, and started a family in Chicago.

I was visiting every other month, but this wasn't my vision. I wanted us to be close. I said, "We are moving to Chicago." I'm a Taurus, I go with my horns through walls, if necessary. I hate to depend on anybody.

When I announced I was moving, my friends thought I was crazy. My salon was doing well, but money isn't my priority; my kids are number one. I'm raised family oriented. I want to visit regularly and see grandkids growing. My husband said I was crazy; I told him that he could stay if he wanted.

After we moved from Pennsylvania to Illinois to be close to my daughter and the grandkids, that's when I started to feel lonely. Because my husband is a very jealous person. He thinks that everybody is looking at me. There could be a crowd of thousands of people or a crowd of five. He thinks that everybody is looking at me. That everybody desires me. When I was at home with my husband, [I felt lonely]. I didn't have my network; I left everything. [You must] keep your mind in different directions. If I'm only by myself with him, my mind (it's not our friend, and could be our worst enemy) would drive me crazy.

Before we moved to Illinois, we had friends. We threw parties often. I had people I communicated with. And we bought a house our second year after we [moved]. I started having people come over. I had huge parties. I love to cook, and I cook everything from scratch. When the weather was nice, I would have parties every weekend. I felt good because I love to be around people. I love to feel their presence and talk to them. After [parties] he would start in about [how a certain man] could not take their eyes off me. [My husband] creates his fantasy; we realized later [he is unwell]. When I reflect on our life in Bulgaria, I can see now that this was in front of us, but nobody did anything. That was a taboo. We tried to help him. He needs help, but he doesn't listen.

When we moved to Philadelphia, we wanted to find Bulgarians. We learned how to walk and talk and live when we arrived. We needed a community of Bulgarians to seek help and advice. When we moved to Illinois, he didn't need that help. He doesn't have friends. He's probably lonely. It's sad. He probably had difficulty during childhood. He's not a tall man. His mom told us they started to look for a doctor to understand why he was "little" and did not grow. She was a big part of his insecurity. His mom told him he was little and not big enough.

Eight years in Chicago, no friends at all. We had one couple from the same city in Bulgaria, we were together a couple of times. But my husband loves to play psychologist. He will tell you what you like, hate, etc. People don't like that. He loves to analyze everybody. And we lost lots of people because of that. Nobody likes that. He tried to keep me away from people and didn't want to share me with anybody. We didn't go anywhere. I felt like I lived in a cave with my husband except when I [visited] my kids or they visited, or at work.

Author: He's not jealous, then, when you are by yourself with him?

Val: Yes. That's when I started realizing that he thinks that I am his belonging or his property, [when] I try to meet with other people. We [my family] would get together four times a year and that's it. I am not that type of person. I love to be with people; I love to talk. Being [only] with him watching television [was not good]. I'm not a fan of watching television. When I'm at home—I love soft jazz—I listen to music—that's what I do. I read books to keep myself busy.

Author: What if you didn't keep yourself busy?

Val: Then I would probably go insane. I love to be busy. I'm a person on the move.

Author's Note: I asked Val to describe her marriage and rate her loneliness.

Val: My husband is controlling; so is his mother. I was lonely when I was with my husband. Don't forget, I work a lot. I'm with people a lot.

Author: How would you rate loneliness now?

Val: With my children, never lonely. With my husband, always lonely. With friends at work, never lonely. My loneliest [is] when I am with him; he complains a lot. I'm not a complainer. When we are watching the news, he starts bitching about this or that, and it drains my energy. That's my loneliness. And I can't argue with him; if I say something, he will say, "You don't know!" He will criticize me, always. There was a long period of time he would call me names—which I'm not—at all.

It makes me so happy when my clients tell me they love their hair. It makes me feel useful. I can do something for people because I love people. None of my clients call me names, or criticize me, or [tell me] how I should do something. My kids tell me there's no one else on Earth like me, that I am so patient. Unfortunately, I put them through situations I should not have. I was too young in the beginning. From the beginning, it's been this way.

Author: How would you describe the quality of your marriage on a scale from 1 to 5?

Val: Two. Living in my old country as a newlywed, I realized what type of person my husband was in our second year of marriage. In my old country of Bulgaria, leaving your husband or divorcing was out of the question. The custom when married was to live with your husband's parents in one house. Few could afford to own their own place. Living there with my dominating mother-in-law and husband, I was trapped.

I had no choice. We want to make choices, but I didn't have that privilege. I already had a baby. You don't talk about your situations. He started being abusive—oh my God, very early. He hit me a few times—really bad—and I had to put on some makeup.

She [her mother-in-law] would always be between us. She would encourage me to wait till my husband was less angry [to talk with him]. One time I had to spend three days in the attic; I couldn't go out. She said to [my husband] "You don't even watch how you hit her. Hit her somewhere people can't see."

It was rough. And I would have to put my smile on in front of my kids. After many years, they told me what they heard. My son (especially) would pray that [visitors] would stay longer because he knew what would happen after that. I was so in love with my husband that I couldn't see many signs. I just tried to make it work. [Now] I'm happy by myself; honestly, I'm scared to go into another relationship. I don't want to take any chances. Who knows what the future holds?

Author's Note: Val's phone rings. It's her husband. She doesn't answer. He calls again. She takes the call. We resume the interview.

Val: I never talked back to him in Europe, but when we moved here, I didn't have her [mother-in-law] as a judge anymore, so I could start doing something by myself trying to save our marriage. My daughter was a very good student, and to this day, my husband is never happy. No matter what you do, he will never say, "Good. That was a good job you did." Or "I'm proud of you." or anything like that. Never. Never. [When her daughter was young] he started talking to her, saying, "You'll be nothing." And that's when I jumped twice and told him not to talk to my daughter like that anymore. You don't talk to somebody like that because you make that little person believe what you are saying [about them]. I had the nerve to stand in front of him.

In nearly twenty years of living with his parents, he never stood up for me—except once. We were going to visit his mother's family [in Bulgaria]. I was wearing a denim skirt a little above my knees. We lived on the third level. We were coming downstairs, and she said to me, "You're going to my family looking like that? With that short skirt?

You're a married woman with a child." I didn't know what to say. My husband said, "What, her legs are not

straight enough? She has a beautiful body. That skirt is not short. It's an okay skirt." And they had an argument. That one time [he stood up for me], that was it.

Author: I shifted the discussion to present day. Val lives separately from her husband in southwest Florida. She fell in love with Florida during a visit; after nine years in Chicago, she decided to move. Her two children and their families live in Chicago.

Val: [About her grandchildren:] She is a teenager, and he is a tween. I felt bad for having to leave them, but then I put my life in perspective. At the end of the day, I'm a life person. I need my life. I can always visit. I moved here and have been happy since. A little after the move, I announced [to my husband] "I am done. I don't want to live with you anymore. I want to breathe. I want my peace. I want to be in peace, and I'm not when I am with you." We lived together in a house like roommates; me in one room and him in another. Our intimate life finished [long ago].

He didn't understand. He asked me "How long do you need?" I said, "What do you mean how long do I need? Forever. Till I die. I want to be by myself." I made a deal with him that if he returned to our apartment in Europe, I would pay for him to move. He said, "Okay." I could not believe it. He flew to Bulgaria on the day Hurricane Ian hit. He asked me if I wanted him to come back. "No," I told him. "Go." I was so naïve.

A few weeks later, my daughter asked, "How long do you think he will last?" I said, "What do you mean? I pay him to stay there. Is that not enough?"

She said, "Mom, are you really that naïve? Of course, he'll come. He will never leave you. He will never, ever leave you. The only way for you [to have peace] is to disappear."

Author: He wants control?

Val: He wants to breathe down my neck. I will never get divorced. In January, he texted me he was returning to the States, and the hair on my skin stood up. He has no friends here. He came back in February. He stayed with the kids and finished projects for them. He would do anything for them.

Author: Do you feel less lonely here in Florida than in Chicago? Does his presence and calls affect you negatively? If so, what is that like?

Val: Yes, I feel less lonely in Florida than in Chicago. His presence does affect me negatively. I feel like he's stalking me. I know he's capable of that. When I asked him why he returned [and ruined our plan to make money in retirement because he's now living in the rental home], he said he was bored. I can't argue or fight with him. We have property together. I don't have the power anymore to fight. My point is, when I am old, I don't want to rely on anybody. I want to rely on myself. I can't be a burden on my kids; that would kill me. I want to be in peace; I don't want to hear any [of his] complaints or cursing. I want to hear nothing.

Author: What motivates you to keep going?

Val: My personality; my kids.

Author: Can you explain more about what you mean by "your personality?"

Val: I'm a Taurus; I believe in signs. I'm a fighter; I'm a fire. I don't give up. I will give up if I try something for long enough and it's pointless. I came to the United States without hope. I came and thought that I would do anything possible to get away from my mother-in-law and to give my kids a better chance. I keep going. I am not satisfied until I am satisfied.

Author: What do you do when you feel lonely? How do you manage it?

Val: When I was forced to be with my husband after work, or on days off, I would visit my kids, read, or kill time. I did anything possible to put my mind somewhere else. I have a good ability to ignore noise around me. But after years, it gets harder to ignore. I try not to absorb the words coming from his mouth. I want complete peace.

Now I can make decisions. Many years ago, I couldn't. I was not allowed. Now I make my decisions. Are they right ones? I don't know. Maybe I need to read and discover more about how to better handle my situation.

Author's Note: We wrapped up the interview discussing coping mechanisms, and I asked her to explain why she hesitates to use the Internet to find resources for coping. I asked her to share with me what she relies on to make decisions.

Val: Honestly? I use my inner voice, meditate, and practice mindfulness. Or, if it's not related to my relationship with my husband, I will talk to my kids as they are my biggest supporters. I will seek their opinion. I can't expect them to "take sides." He's still their father. I trust them

1,000%. I know what I want; I know that I love doing hair. I've done it for so many years and never get tired of it. I've started a real estate business for when I start getting aches and pains. I see myself in the future as a real estate agent. If I'm healthy enough, I can be an agent until I am 85. I don't expect my kids to take care of me unless I have no choice. Quite the reverse: If I can help, I will help them.

Author: It seems you grew in confidence to say "No" after moving to the United States.

Val: I have always been confident. But in Bulgaria, because of the culture, I didn't have choices. They didn't understand me. All my life I've been confident. I realized that I couldn't do anything back then because of the culture. I had to clench my teeth and keep going. I had my salon and was successful. When I visited Bulgaria after eleven years, people still recognized me, "You haven't changed a bit!"

I strongly believe that I know myself enough to know what I expect and what I'm capable of. You can't have your vision with something that is literally not possible to achieve. I always go with the simple and possible things in front of me. And I'm trying to accomplish them. It takes patience, more than anything else.

Author's Note: Personality affects how people process and manage loneliness. Some people can manage it because of personality characteristics. Persons who are shy, reserved, self-deprecating, or don't know themselves experience greater loneliness than persons who are extroverted or more confident. The more we learn ourselves, the more likely we reach a point where loneliness is not a huge, heavy burden. Building confidence in our inner voice builds resiliency. When we better understand ourselves, we pursue needs to bring fulfillment. I learn what I love and what I don't love. If I am doing something unmotivated by who I am and what I want, that doesn't make me happy, and I'm disconnected from myself. Loneliness is the difference between what we need and have, and what we desire. Loneliness is that gap. We cannot change all things that bring loneliness—loss of a loved one, for instance. However, we can address our feelings, discuss them with a trusted person, and choose to align ourselves with healthy behaviors to lessen lonely feelings.

Val: I was lonely for so many years, and I knew exactly what I was doing to myself. From the beginning, I thought that I had no right to leave my kids without a father. I thought about divorcing him. Honestly, I never cared what people thought about me. If I want your opinion about my dress, I'll ask you for that. But other than that, I don't care what people think about me. When you see reality, it's possible, it's achievable, and you go after it. It can't happen overnight. I know how hard I work to accomplish.

STRATEGIES TO ↓ LONELINESS

MINDFULNESS

Pay attention to the present without judgment.

TALK THERAPY

Speak w/ a trusted friend or therapist.

INCLUSION

Create & maintain a safe & healthy environment.

LIVASH

THE GREAT EMPTY
Carmel, Indiana

DECEMBER 2013

He was precious and handsome, and she glowed with exhausted fatigue. She had birthed a beautiful son. His shock of black hair and chestnut eyes glistened. She, though worn, grinned. Joy emanated from her being through weariness from hours in labor and delivery. I beamed, yet my heart wrestled with the bittersweet. Unexpectedly, like a summer thunderstorm, I stifled the flood of tears threatening downpour. I could not release them, not now. This was her time of joy, not a resurrection of my pain. To this day, I'm unsure why the birth of her son surfaced the empty sadness. Perhaps it was the proximity of our ages. Perhaps it was the weight of disenchantment in marriage, or the inevitable "ripening" of my reproductive system. Pangs of an empty womb and withered romance groaned in the deep recesses of my mind. I breathed and smiled as she held him close, truly happy for her happiness.

It's been a decade since that cold, wintry evening, yet vivid are the images from wrestling the ache of emptiness. With tear-stained cheeks, I drove south towards home, lonely in heart, and alone yet again. He was doing something somewhere; he was absent from most events. We lived, for all intents and purposes, separate lives. Among family, it became "normal" that he wasn't with me. At first, I felt shame and embarrassment heat my face with their questions. But with time, I callused to their questions. Inquiries lessened. I numbed.

I was married on paper, yet relationally single, chained by a promise to a man who only sometimes participated in life with me. As I turned onto the quiet road exiting the hospital that night, I examined the weight of emptiness upon my heart—I was childless and unhappily married. I couldn't do anything about either condition—or so I thought. The well of loneliness deepened. I was losing a marriage from apathy with a personality my opposite, and helpless in the baby department too. Though adoption surfaced in polite conversation, I wasn't interested in bringing a child into a marriage void of passion and weak in emotional connection.

The specialist advised me six years earlier not to bear children; with that diagnosis, I'd made my decision. I can't bring a child into this world with a 50% chance of inheriting a genetic disorder. I harbored doubts: Would I be a good mom? What if I failed? But time marches on, and if we want, we change and grow. And the decrees we speak in naïve youth disintegrate in the fire of maturity. Brutal is the ache, and deep is the loneliness when life's moments (like births) slap you in the face, reminding you of your Great Empty. A wellspring of grief through tears carried me home like a leaf on a river.

We must process the grief of loss, even if the loss has never inhabited consciousness. We must grieve the loss of hope in wishes that did not, and will not, come to fruition as dreamed. We must feel through the pain. We must also find a supportive network—at least one soul—to whom we can pour out the pain of loneliness. This process is critical to lessening its intensity, reframing our perspective, and building resiliency.

NOTE TO SELF
Indianapolis, Indiana

JUNE 11, 2014

Move, speak, and act like you love yourself.
What would it look like for me if I did?

GABLE
Solo drive to Savannah, GA

THANKSGIVING WEEKEND, 2014

I booked a solo vacation to visit Savannah; I decided to drive (all thirteen hours) to save money. He was working, per usual. I needed a break, with or without him. I was looking forward to exploring a new place; I needed space. Our frayed bond was weakening and suffered another blow to its integrity the night before I departed for Georgia, the night we lost our blue boy.

Gable did not like baths; like me, he hated water in his ears. Post-bath zoomies around the house included some form of racing and a squeaky toy. This time was no different; yet while cleaning the tub, I heard him shout—something was wrong. I jolted up from my crouched position and rounded the hall to look over the banister. I watched Gable spasm in his chair, writhing to breathe and coordinate his movements. I raced down the stairs, grabbed him as best I could despite contracting limbs, and pulled him to my lap. As I sat against the cold, tile floor, restraining him from self-harm, spasming limbs tore a hole in my tights as he struggled.

He watched as I cradled Gable, his taut muscles gasping for air. Within a minute, limbs went limp from the fatigue. To feel my blue boy so lethargic brings tears to my eyes. We sat in shock; Gable's ribcage barely rose with the shallowest of breaths. He smelled of clean apple, his fur shining. The drive to the emergency vet was short. We carried Gable, docile with exhaustion, into the office, bewilderment straining our faces. The vet kept it simple: it was time. He likely passed a blood clot, and the episode would happen again.

Weeks before, Gable attempted to clear a fence rail. Before we could intervene, he came up short, knocking the rail with the base of his wide ribcage, causing a deep purple bruise to form. He kept running, apparently unphased. It's only when the veterinarian said he likely suffered a blood clot that we put two and two together.

One of the few times I recall seeing him cry is that night, as Gable breathed his last shallow breaths lying on the cold examination table, wrapped in his blanket. We felt his acute loss with piercing pain. I imagine we each felt it more profoundly, separately. Gable was an amazing dog, a former show whippet—tall, elegant, blue-brindled, and beaming with spontaneity. He was my heart dog, and, if I were to guess, his too.

ICEBERG

Indianapolis, Indiana

2015

No matter what I do, I can't get at you, and it's your soul that I want.[22]

I rolled over, and in the twilight felt his warmth, noting how the faint light illuminated shoulders that retained tone, even in deep sleep. Unrequited desire ached to merge our bodies, to tuck in and rest in the strength of his form. I hesitated. I wanted to caress his smooth, hardened skin. Yet fear stifled desire—fear of the same rejection. Frozen by a flood of feeling, I merely observed. He was turned away from me. Always turned away, always a space between us. Whether in flesh or soul, on the couch or in bed, cool, empty space secured shotgun.

Yet, hope reigned supreme. As air exited my lungs, I scooched in to snuggle against his smooth skin. Empty silence slapped my senses. No response. My mind screamed, *Don't you want me? I'm your dearly beloved, the one you promised to love and cherish until death parts us! I'm trying, can't you see? Can't you feel?* The silence of a thousand tiny rejections echoed in my chest.

Did he know my heart existed? Or did I exist merely to check a metaphorical box? As a couple, we looked the part. We were tall, athletic, and educated. He was brown-haired; I was blonde. We were balanced—or so it appeared. Yet beneath the shining smiles that required years to straighten, and with carefully crafted civility, *We* were an empty shell: without feeling, without warmth, without hope. Like a wounded alley cat, I withdrew to my side of the bed, though my heart plaintively beckoned for even a morsel of response. My love barometer dropped lower by the day, creeping inevitably towards a storm.

HIS NOTE
Indianapolis, Indiana

UNDATED

I want you to know, despite the pain and hurt that resurfaces, I forgive you and love you with all my heart. Please forgive me of my complacent attitude and not having my heart in it to meet your emotional needs.

EDIFICATION
Nashville, Indiana

OCTOBER 9, 2015

People need to see humble confidence in achievement, strength, and growth.

A CRY FROM WITHIN

Downtown Indianapolis, Indiana

DECEMBER 31, 2015

Our bond ruptured that night. Its weakening throughout the years of passionless matrimony primed it for dissolution in the face of the ultimate test of support—crisis.

I recall the stillness in the room as his body churned within to heal—to save itself from oblivion. I stood to his left, staring at his electrode-covered head. He was unaware of my presence; I observed. Scenes from that evening are imprinted into my senses as if I could reach out and feel the hum and warm heat created by machines monitoring his system of systems.

Everyone held their breath. I was alone and feeling lonely; but loneliness had to wait. Anger cut in line hours before as my mind usurped the reins from my heart, pounding its gavel in defiant decision. Pacing the family waiting room in the wee hours of New Year's Day, we collectively wrung hands in suspended grief as the youngest fought for his life in the ICU.

He was absent. The unspoken question reflected in their eyes, "Where is he? Why isn't he here with you?" One person flew the red eye 2,000 miles to be present. Yet he was likely asleep in our bed less than ten miles north. Anger, fueled by sadness, grew hot within, and I knew then I would never receive the support I needed to live a vibrant life together. I grieved, but urgency directed my attention to the matter at hand—would he survive the night?

Loneliness is one of the most toxic environmental conditions we can encounter.

— Steve Cole
UCLA

LIGHTENING

Driving south on Michigan Road, Indianapolis, Indiana

JANUARY 2016

As weary in spirit as the sky was gray and rainy, I rolled to the stoplight at the corner of Michigan and 38th Street. I recall the red light in my field of vision. I was starting over; I reminded myself not to mourn the loss of a nine-year role with one company. They had, after all, been purchased and sold multiple times in recent years and had recently filed for bankruptcy. No wonder they laid off the former President and me. I was grateful to be employed with a salary, benefits, and, most important, medical care. It didn't matter that I was overqualified for the new job, didn't feel mentally challenged, or that people were resigning from that department left and right. I was gainfully employed and needed to finish law school.

It came from nowhere—the worst pain I'd ever felt. Thankfully, I made it through the intersection and kept driving, though all I could feel was excruciating pain. It's as if an ice pick had been jabbed into my right temple, through my eye, and straight to the middle of my head behind my nose. My eye twitched, I teared up, my nose leaked, and facial muscles spasmed. It lasted about thirty seconds then cleared like mist with the morning sun's rays.

My head had been aching on the right side—a low, dull throb—for well over a year. I'd noticed the intensifying pressure, but never did lightning strike my temple as it did that morning. After that day, however, lightning strikes became the norm—though only in the sense that they didn't go away completely. I could never tell when the flash of pain would hit, though I began to note triggers when the pressure built, the ice pick jabbed, and my eye would twitch then tear. I tried to explain it to loved ones. I sought doctors who prescribed medications, yet nothing touched this pain.

ABANDONED
Indianapolis, Indiana

2016

Maybe he'll respond this time. I stepped from the shower, grabbed my towel, and tentatively approached. He wore only shorts this summer evening as he made the bed while the sun shone warmly through the west-facing windows of our bedroom. Naked, I towel-dried my hair and approached his fit, warm body from behind, wrapping my arms around his waist, pressing my chest into the muscles of his back. He froze.

No acknowledgment. No caress. No warmth in return. He didn't even turn around. Like a Roomba that runs into an obstacle, he paused for a moment—bedsheet midair—adjusted his body to insert space between his back and my belly, and resumed making the bed. That moment broke me. It branded pain into memory, into every fiber of my female heart. Silently, and robotic-like in response, I turned from him, dressed, and descended the stairs to prepare dinner.

What a metaphor for loneliness—wet, naked, and vulnerable, reaching out to connect—only to receive rejection. Never had a centimeter of space felt more like a chasm between our hearts. Hell, I didn't know his heart, even after a decade of marriage. He rarely spoke of feelings, and if pressed to discuss them, more silence and distance were the fruits of my labors. I wanted desperately to actively love him, to be the one he let into his heart. Why promise to be there for the other if you can't share emotions? Yet no effort on my part could overcome strong roots of stoic silence.

Encounters like these had become commonplace as I improved my own communication. Four rounds of couples counseling in twelve years taught me skills to employ when life hit hard. Through pain, uncertainty, and work, I awakened to the harm I caused by reacting instead of responding. Reacting was the default programming of my upbringing. Like a freshly born foal, I awkwardly learned to first process my emotions, then use words to inquire for further understanding. As we matured into our thirties, however, our relationship did not strengthen. We did grow, but not together. We applied principles learned in therapy, yet grew apart. Perhaps we each grew into ourselves. Living out our "homework" from therapists became elementary in method. But with continuing failed attempts to connect, my emotions roiled.

I became an expert in suppressing my responses so as not to rock the boat. I redoubled efforts to be a good Christian girl who always accommodated and put others' needs before my own. I was to submit to him, right? We stood in front of friends and family and promised to love one another as God loved us; to honor the other, in body and soul. As the years passed, however, I knew deeply within that our love was not the kind of love I needed. I knew our love did not express the brilliance of what love could reflect. Our love, by contrast, had grown thorny and brittle. A thread of repeated rejections meandered its way through the fabric of our days. Our communication became contrived and incongruent. It honored neither of us. We were dying; we didn't even act as friends.

After a predictable dinner, I approached him. My heart raced as it garnered strength to speak, to be vulnerable and ask for what it needed. I poured out my heart, canvassing my emotions. I wanted to be with him; to share with him; to love him. Yet I felt alone lying next to him. I desired to bridge the gap. I wanted to make *Us* work; I made a commitment and wasn't ready to throw in the towel—ever. Yet I needed his affection. How much effort did it take to make someone see? I was yearning—trying so damn hard to get a reaction—to receive something (breadcrumbs would have sufficed!) for my efforts to build intimacy. Not enough, as it turns out.

To this outpouring I received an admission: He knew I wanted to be intimate when I embraced him, but he couldn't be bothered. He wanted to shower and eat dinner. The schedule had to be followed, and my invitation to take me on our freshly cleaned sheets simply wasn't in the schedule. My chest tightened, stomach churned, and hopes collapsed.

CHRONIC LONELINESS LEADS TO INCREASED RISKS FOR:

Alcoholism

Memory loss

Depression

Anxiety

Suicidal thoughts

Illness

Obesity

Sleeplessness

Early death

♡ disease

LivAsh

WHAT IF?
Indianapolis, Indiana

2016

It creeps in. But does It?

Candidly, warning signs surfaced with regular cadence. At first, they whispered, *Stop. Breathe. Reassess. Slow down. Listen. Do something.*

Then louder, *Slow down. Listen, please.*

And finally, *Stop! Listen.*

I stopped to listen, eventually. Hindsight broadens our view. In widescreen mode, we can see the pockmarked landscape of our souls: a cratered field where traumas, busy schedules, and years of ignoring needs lead to brush fires that engulfed our capacities but did not destroy us. Yet, fires are still hot.

Fires burn.

Fires consume.

It's easy to ignore the small ways we allow precious life to leak away, like a drip from a faucet, unless we are mindful and practice stillness. Because when stillness exists, even a drip lands in the sink like a gong.

I noticed It driving east on Interstate 465. I was tired after eight hours working full-time followed by four hours—five nights a week—sitting in colorless classrooms learning the law. As I signaled to exit the highway, the thought sailed across my visage like a ghostly pirate ship on a moonless night.

It would be quick. It would be painless, and then It would be over. And the relentless pain in my temple and the ache of loss in my gut would end. I would no longer crawl towards kindness like a desert-weathered refugee yearns for water. I would be free of both pain and loneliness, and then I could breathe. With one sharp turn of the steering wheel into the pylon of the bridge, my Honda would crush like a can, and me too. I couldn't hit one of the water cans though—that would diminish the impact.

What the hell are you thinking?!? Reason slapped me with fury, and the deathly ghosts evaporated.

Whoa! What is happening? Consciousness echoed.

I shook off the thought; anxiety filled the gap: I was almost home. In recent months, *home* had frozen into an iceberg of emotionless stoicism. I ached for the welcome of warm hugs and conversation yet expected nothing. Depressing disappointment defeated hope. Perhaps I'd be greeted warmly, perhaps not. More than likely, however, I'd receive more of the same—routine. We'd go through the motions: He'd say "Hey" from the couch while watching sports or playing a video game, and I'd unload my gear from a twelve-hour day like a battle-hardened soldier; kiss his forehead or rub his shoulder; then plod upstairs for a cry in the shower.

Anxiety-ridden evenings grew fat as law school steam-rolled my brain into submission. Without the exercise of emotional expression, our evenings, our communication, and our marriage weakened into uselessness. An emptiness settled into my bones; and with it, more frequent and intensifying ghosts.

Perhaps loneliness is the "maker of the soul" as Emily Dickinson wrote. Taking measure of it in the dark recesses of your being profoundly shocks your system. Perhaps—had I heeded the calls of loneliness sooner, addressed my own needs, and faced fears while speaking with a professional—I would not have found myself debating death in the bathtub.

It would be so easy, so painless, and I'd be free to breathe. I could avoid that pain—that awful, barren pain of rejection. A small cut in hot water is a more elegant means to depart than ramming my car into the overpass. I pondered this as my toes surfaced the waterline while my aching back and shoulder soaked in the scalding water. A hot bath in a quiet home with candles—while soothing and relaxing—is also dreamlike. At that time, in my state of mind and tortured soul, the bathroom became the sea. The warm water, candles, and fragrant salts called to me like sirens calling to Odysseus. I could feel the tug of their calls, promising peace, and a warm embrace.

What the hell? Snap out of it! Reason reached into the water and yanked me back to the safety of shore.

I sat upright, startled by these machinations, and wept. I don't recall if he was upstairs, downstairs, or even in the house. It's immaterial. The travesty is that not only was I contemplating ending my life, lulled by the siren of suicide, but that I knew I couldn't share with him that I was having these thoughts. I did not feel emotional safety. It was hopeless; rejection would prevail. Emptiness dawned, and Lonely turned her face towards it, like a flower to the sun.

A therapist once reassured me that everyone has suicidal thoughts, that their mere existence does not mean an emergency exists. I found encouragement in his words yet knew such thoughts would resurface without action. That slow drip was increasing; the signal to act slapped me in the face. I listened and knew the cost of action. It would fundamentally alter my life. Action meant stopping the drip yet ending the marriage.

NUMB
Fishers, Indiana

DECEMBER 2016

"You need a man who's gonna slap your ass and make you laugh." He said it with nonchalance during our holiday dinner. I stared at him. I was alone; my other half was once again absent from the festivities. The rest of the family quieted, ready for the next move. They knew and agreed, yet never shared that with me. Whatever. Apathy reigned while shame took the back seat. Liv was lost and lonely. They knew; so did I.

FEEL THROUGH IT
Indiana

SPRING 2017

I recall in memory the event that switched on the floodlights within my soul and shouted, "Awaken!" I'd held on to hope like a child dragging their tattered blankie. Divorce was imminent. I carried the oppressive, anvil-heavy burden upon my chest leading to that day. I starved my heart for years, living on scraps of affection; but within weeks of one weekend, I had filed for divorce. I finally chose me after years of sacrificing myself to the zephyr-like altar of "happily ever after." When I started over, I started living.

Knowledge is power, and the only way out is through. To manage pain and loneliness, I have learned to observe what I feel; *feel through it;* and keep going. The heavy lifting of feeling through it occurred only after I chose myself. I chose to live, and this meant leaving a marriage void of true emotional connection and passion. Years of frozen feelings and disappointed attempts to awaken true affection precipitated within me a negative self-esteem spiral. I arrived at a crossroads of choice—a bedraggled shell of self—faced with grasping at life or succumbing to sadness. As foreign as it felt to choose me at that time, my Knower knew it was the necessary step. I had too long avoided the Pandora's Box of painful emotional injuries festering in my chest. Instinct whispered to me: I must open the box. I decided to listen to the messages my body and mind screamed into the void.

With a sense of urgency spawned by thinning hair and bald patches, I applied well-being principles learned in graduate school to my behaviors. The doctor ordered blood tests. Adrenal fatigue. My body was shutting down from trying to keep itself together without listening, without resting, and without honoring myself. My physical pain was ablaze and my emotional pain frantic. My blood was low on several vitamins and minerals. Due to birth control and emotional eating, I'd gained weight.

My training as an exercise scientist and health educator awakened with focused precision. Pain screamed for attention; instead of numbing it with cheap medications, I chose to listen. I chose to learn how my body felt each morning—how did my joints feel when I did this movement? How did my whole person, body and mind, respond to familiar relationship patterns? It was a hard, solo journey through the wasteland of want, yet enlightening. Knowledge is power. Learning strengthened my will. Every forward step bred confidence to choose what I inherently knew: that I was worthy of living a life I loved, even if I lived it alone.

GREAT EXPECTATIONS
Indianapolis, Indiana

SUMMER 2017

He didn't even look at me. He merely stood, mechanically washing the dishes.

Emotional recall is vivid; I could paint a picture of that evening's imagery, twelve years before. The details, however, wane with time. Three years—we waited three years to unify our physical bodies and "become one." Driven by the fear of eternal separation from God (as only religion can instill), we "saved ourselves" for our wedding night. I thought he wanted me; at least, that's the message I received until a few months before the wedding. I was grievously mistaken. I brushed off his changed behavior in the months leading to the altar, ignoring the whispered warnings of intuition that something was off. My self-esteem was shit, and so any number of excuses for the waning connection seemed plausible. Maybe it was the distance. Maybe it was the new job. Maybe it was stress. Maybe it was moving. Maybe, maybe, maybe.

There was no connection that night—no fireworks to bask in, no landscapes to explore, no waves to ride. No joy. No laughter. No safety in learning-as-you-go. Expectation is a swindler, preying upon hopes and dreams, using wounds to claw at your soul. Was it unreasonable to expect intimacy on our wedding night? There was no party, no alcohol, and no fanfare. No reason, in short, for a lack of interest. The ceremony was a quiet affair—too quiet. I had once again settled for less than my intuition knew, constricted by budget, expectations, and weak self-esteem. Didn't he want to marry me after three years of waiting? Had I been so blind as to choose a man who could not express?

Alas, twelve years later, as he stood at the kitchen sink, bare-chested in his athletic shorts and handsome as ever, he stated, "I wasn't ready to marry you." Astonishment shook my soul. He said it as if I—*We*—meant nothing. He was angry. Who could blame him? I had filed for divorce weeks before and moved out as soon as I found suitable housing.

As tears poured first from my soul and then from my eyes, he continued to disclose with nonchalance. He had wanted the big wedding with the rehearsal dinner, music, and dancing. I listened with surprise and spoke nothing. In twelve years of sleeping in the same bed, he never shared these desires. He did, however, clarify that he "did his part" by buying me a diamond engagement ring. He would contribute no more funds to wedding preparation. This was yet another warning light I let blink unattended, because I didn't think I'd find another man who would want me. The separation of loneliness existed before we exchanged vows.

His truths shredded my soul as they sideswiped me, a helpless, bewildered fledgling on the road, unsure which way to go as traffic whizzed. Despite my best efforts to understand, complete with inquiries and a river of tears, I received little explanation. Lonely desperation enveloped me. Defeated, I picked up the shredded pieces of what remained of my heart and walked out of the recently remodeled kitchen for the last time.

LOVE-SHAPED HOLE
Indianapolis, Indiana

AUTUMN 2017

Dammit! It would not budge. It creaked, cracked, and skidded against the layers of poorly painted trim as I struggled to raise it. I heaved. Tears welled in my eyes. Then I cracked the glass. I dropped to the floor, splayed out on the freshly installed, fluffy carpet that smelled of glue. I wept like a baby whose toy was taken from their hand.

All I could think about was the ease with which they opened—gliding along with a mere finger to guide them. Sparkling, shiny, and new. I could clean them without craning my neck or aggravating carpal tunnel. They locked with a sure, swift turn and kept the space nice and temperate. I missed them—and the thousands of dollars spent to install them. I released a frustrated, stifled scream, took a breath, then cried. Divorce sucks.

Empty grief landed on my chest, and I sobbed on the floor of my rental, an aging cottage with original windows that refused to open. I had traded a freshly remodeled, 2,200-sq.-ft. home for 750 square feet of creaking floors, inoperable windows, and minimal storage space. Bawling resumed with renewed energy. I reminded myself, however, in that scene of domestic frustration, that I was now free from fear, and safe in the surety that I could start over with time and tenacity. I wondered if I would ever love again—and if so, would I receive love in return? Healing had started, and it was messy. Yet, I no longer watched my life in grayscale but was the author of my story. Like any great rom-com, the protagonist was up to her elbows untying life's knots in comedic, character-building scenarios.

Crisis averted and courage mustered, I popped up from my weeping position. In a classic MacGyver move, I scavenged several pieces of wood to prop open the windows as far as each would permit. That would do; life was waiting.

ENCOURAGEMENT
Indianapolis, Indiana

CHRISTMAS EVE, 2017

You are a friend to all people.
You've got strength to know in your Knower.
Trust yourself to structure, foundation, and discipline.
Feel it all; come alive to life. You've been on pause for so long.
Cream rises to the top in whatever circumstances.
Be yourself. Be true to you. It will work out.
Shine your light.

GROWING PAINS

Indianapolis, Indiana

WINTER 2018

The past informs your present but does not predict your future. I wrote this sentiment with a dry-erase marker on my mirror one crisp morning as I prepared for the exhausting schedule of the day ahead: work, school, study. Freshly divorced from a twelve-year marriage and tending my wounded soul, I taught adults in the city while wrangling toxicity in my work environment. I followed this daily fight by learning law as a third-year evening student.

I attempted to mask with foundation not only bodily aches and pains etched on my face, but the pain of emotional loss revealed by dark crescents under my eyes. I "saw" the woman staring back at me; I paused. I sensed hope and resolve. I would make it through this heart pain, just as I had this past decade, through pain from surgery after surgery. I felt strong despite the void left by terminating a long-term relationship. My body ached this frosty morning, and so did my weary heart. I reflected on events within the ten years since receiving the Ehlers-Danlos diagnosis. I was alone and learning a new home and neighborhood. And yet, I felt a freedom of spirit. My soul craved a safe space, and in this creaky old home, I was building it.

The path before me held potential; uncertain endings existed, but opportunities bloomed. I had turned a corner in managing chronic pain two years earlier—and because I no longer lived in the emptiness of indecision, I was finally stepping into my life as its director. I had rejected all pain medication. I cautiously befriended what I believed; I practiced what I intuitively knew as the healing power of nutrition and movement. I knew my body and heart could recover from the brink. Choosing myself was no longer a cripplingly shameful act but one of growing grace—an acceptance of being a worthy human. Acceptance of myself, my needs, and my desires was necessary to accomplish all I dreamt.

As I saw myself in the mirror for what felt like the first time, I knew the present trials would serve as a crucible to develop strength. Instead of branding me a failure, the past transformed into a well of knowledge, deep with wisdom that only experiences teach. Crucibles crush; yet through heat and pressure, they change their cargo, purifying it to its essentials. And in such intense change, crucibles are instruments of creation.

The past informs your present but does not predict your future. I often speak this aloud, especially in moments when fear, frustration, or loss whisper in my mind. The concept catapults forward movement in the face of their clamoring. The phrase canvasses the journey of joys and tribulations inherent in living a human existence. We cannot undo the past; we cannot predict the future. We can only *ever* exist in the present. And when we practice mindfulness, the "practice of being present," loneliness lessens. Instead of ruminating on the space between what we don't have and all we desire, we allow gratitude for what we do have at that time.

ALL APOLOGY

Fishers, Indiana

JULY 2018

Amid the cheers and laughter, I exited via the back door. Walking the fence rail, I listened. "I am sorry for being a crappy husband; I did not have the capacity to love you the way you needed to be loved." I cried; I listened. I wiped the tears to disguise the ache of my heart from hearing the words it knew were true all those years. I returned to the party, mind swimming. Though less cheerful and heart grieving, his apology released a burden I was unaware I still carried.

CONTAINED CHAOS
State Fairgrounds, Indianapolis, Indiana

AUGUST 2018

I wanted to spend time with my family, but I feared the unknown. Few social activities graced my calendar—especially boisterous ones—because pain waged war ruthlessly. I'd been engaged in skirmishes with guerilla tactics and breakthrough pain that brought me to my knees. I felt weary from battle yet yearned for relief amid the hypervigilance of scanning the battlefield, awaiting the next attack of stabbing, burning, piercing pain.

My trepidation had little to do with spending the day with family, and everything to do with the environment: how it felt, and the sounds, smells, and movements within it. My mind recalled in memory what it would be like: a thousand chattering voices erupting around me in unpredictable and piercing cackles, guffaws, shrieks, and shrills. Sound would layer upon sound, forming a glacier, grinding frayed nerves like fingernails against sandpaper. I wanted to avoid the clamor and shoulder-bumping of strangers—my sanity depended upon it. Instead of seeing happy people eagerly waiting in line to order a deep-fried Twinkie, I saw cattle being led to slaughter.

Oblivious to the sweat dripping from their brows, revelers adjusted the sweat-soaked cotton clothing clinging awkwardly to their skin. The state fair was too much—the heat, sweat, and smells—for my senses. I could feel my stomach churning. The relentless ache in my temples was belligerent; I did not want to further irritate it. The smell of elephant ears hit me as I approached the fairgrounds: the sweet combination of aged fat and fluffy dough doused in powdered sugar sickened me. Sounds assaulted my eardrums. I ached to sprint to the nearest patch of shade trees—away from it all—and breathe in the silent, cool air.

I steeled my senses and shifted my gaze from feet to fair. The scene before me painted itself in real time: swaths of people migrated like birds. Many traipsed—mindlessly—from one venue to the next while sweating profusely. None seemed bothered by the languid, shoulder-to-sweaty-shoulder shuffle with strangers.

As my eyes beheld all before me, my stomach soured, heart raced, and sensibilities swirled. Pressure grew within my chest as if an elephant had chosen it for its resting place. Random movements in varying speeds registered in my periphery as blue-lipped children ran ahead of their parents, waiving cotton candy trails behind them.

Movements were both language and chaotic. The mass of humanity roamed. Groups of people, oblivious to everyone, "dropped" into the flow, causing a ripple effect of halts, trips, and curses. Yet within each whirlpool, insensible conversations continued. I could see and hear it all at once, the energy of every person directed towards my senses. My faculties strained at the onslaught. I could discern nothing yet pinpoint the slightest high-pitched squeal of an ecstatic child after their first roller coaster ride. As we crossed the scene, a cacophony of laughter and the low droning of a thousand conversations overwhelmed me. I cracked.

I heaved the humid August air in and out as quickly as I could, though it felt like breathing molasses. I was acutely aware of my posture—hands on knees—to support my lungs, and how it may look to passersby.

I could not breathe.

I could not think.

I could only feel my way through it; the surge of heat ascended from my chest, into my face, and out the top of my head. The pain culminated with the most intense ringing, a sound so piercing I could see it with my third eye. As rapidly and intensely as it arrived, it dissipated into an exquisite silence.

The echoes of pain throbbed in my right ear as I wept bulbous tears into sweaty palms, smearing them across my face as snot dripped from my nose. My Mom stood frozen in observation. Even through my struggle, I felt the weight of responsibility. She didn't know how to act. Crouched behind a state fair food truck near the Midway, her six-foot, former Division I athlete daughter was nearly immobile, except for the distinct sound of belabored breaths between halted outbursts of tears. What comfort could she possibly offer?

I could sense panic-fueled helplessness approach. My breaker had been tripped. Anxiety blossomed. Frustrated fear erupted. These emotions fed seedlings of shame and shook my soul. I felt lonely and broken-beyond-repair. I fumbled for an explanation as exasperation reigned, knowing my ability to handle the stress of social situations was weakening. Vulnerability revealed my bruises, as though I was standing naked in front of a department store mirror, shoppers judging in silence. I grasped for words of explanation, yet none fit the bill. I ached for understanding, but also numbed to sharing my reality. How could anyone understand? I'd become accustomed to the silent confusion from friends and colleagues during a painful episode when my eye would twitch, nose would run, and facial muscles paralyzed. Trapped inside a snow globe of frenzied pain, all could watch, and I could not escape.

Exhaustion overcame me, and I resumed the day's frivolity, though my temple ached from another unpredictable attack of piercing pain. It would be nearly a year until I received a diagnosis.

TIMING IS EVERYTHING
Indianapolis, Indiana

MAY 2019

He walked into my bungalow with a glass-cube flower arrangement from a wholesaler. I took the couch in the cozy dining space, made cheerier by artwork and teal walls the color of north Florida waters at "golden hour." He sat opposite, in my favorite French-tufted, high-backed, velvet chair. Nearly two years had passed since divorce. Weary from long days at work followed by nights finishing law school, I yearned for rest before bar prep began.

He mumbled congratulations on graduating while handing me the glass cube and a small envelope. I mumbled thanks and opened it—a $5 coffee gift card. I refrained from laughter and one of those sighs you make when your internal response is exhausted. *Seriously? After seventeen years of relationship, you gift me a frou-frou coffee and a withering floral arrangement plucked from a pallet with fifty of the same?*

I remained mute, but my body didn't register restraint: defenses rose, and senses sharpened. Why was he here, and what did he want? My eyes and ears focused like lasers on every word and body movement. My choice to attend law school did not, I'm certain, sit well with him. Law school, he once quipped, had "changed me." A visit to my place two years post-divorce on graduation weekend cautioned me. I was prepared to converse, but my heart wasn't ready for his next breath.

"I proposed. We plan to marry next year. Are you dating anyone? You don't want to be alone, do you?"

Whatever I said or did after his news is lost with time. Only a watercolor memory with formless patches of color now remains as I recall the scene. An immediate knot in my stomach formed, and I leaned back slightly as I absorbed the emotional blow to my chest. Pain. Anger. Then realization landed like an anvil at my feet.

Two years earlier, a few weeks after I moved out, he shared that he'd been invited by a female acquaintance to go for a jog. I remember the gravity of surprise as his admission settled into my soul. *He's dating?* I had stopped by our newly remodeled home, one we'd spent countless hours and substantial funds modernizing, to iron out divorce details. With sadness my frequent companion since filing, the sting from his metaphorical slap in my face throbbed. I wrestled with new loneliness as a divorcee, and he was sharing stories of a blossoming romance.

I ignored his slight, offered congratulations, and inquired whether she was more like him in temperament and demeanor. Yes, she was, he said. They approached life similarly. As I processed this news, I thought, *was she a factor in the texting and weekend work he'd been busy with in the months leading to our split?* In twelve years of marriage, I'd rarely seen him text anyone—ever—let alone laugh aloud reading one. He rarely spoke with his best man and, to my knowledge, had no deep friendships. Whether she played a role in his behavior near the end of our marriage is irrelevant. I do not know; it does not matter. I wished him happiness. The memory of his authentic laughter, however, at one such text message, surfaced painful clarity because of its rarity. It carried a cargo of grief and a payload of wasted energy.

THREE'S A CROWD
Indianapolis, Indiana

AUGUST 2019

It's easier said than done, the "just keep swimming" mantra. Sometimes, I want to scream at the sky and cut out the pain that plagues my neck and head when it's at its angriest. Is that too extreme? Perhaps. But the pain is extreme. I've learned that the more intense the pain, the more intense the emotions. Riding ceaseless swells of pain sows seeds that may ripen into extreme solutions—most I've learned to weed without hesitation. Some are suicidal. Yet drastic solutions become viable options when relentless, piercing pain thunders into the body.

In July of 2019, I received the diagnoses of Cluster Headache and Semicircular Canal Dehiscence (SCCD). The former was not curable, only manageable. The latter required cranial surgery to repair. With Cluster Headache, I could only mitigate symptoms. Sadness rushed in hard on the heels of relief. At least I could treat it with a novel medication that was new to the market. When I researched the condition, I felt *seen*.

> "Cluster headache (CH) is arguably the most severe pain condition that afflicts humans. The severity of the pain has earned it the nickname 'suicide headache,' and a suicidal risk exists in this condition. Like other people suffering from chronic pain, CH patients face a double drama in their lives: first, the disease itself, with its attacks of unbearable pain; and second, the difficulty in obtaining high quality medical care, emotional support,

respect, and acceptance, or simply in finding someone who understands how devastating this disease can be. Thus, the life journey of CH patients can be paved with desperate feelings of loneliness, misunderstanding, and mistrust."[23]

SCCD is a rare condition with unknown cause. It occurs when the thin bone separating your brain from your ear anatomy disintegrates, leaving holes that wreak havoc with your balance, vision, hearing, and proprioception. I had complete holes through the bone in my right skull, and thinning bone on the left skull. Given that Cluster Headache affected my right temple, my constant companion was pain—piercing pain from Cluster Headache and aching pain from a hole in my skull. Both worsened upon waking, when staring at a screen, or with too many sounds.

I was offered the option to defer taking the bar exam that August. Yet I chose to take it anyway because I had put in the work. I had volleyed between medications that cause fatigue, irritability, and pain of their own making. I reasoned that if I failed, exam practice would be beneficial.

Keep going anyway.

I finished the bar exam without throwing in the towel or barfing in the bathroom moments before from anxiety and pain. I had studied, cried, read, re-read, recited, and reviewed for weeks. I was absolutely spent. The pressure within my head and neck was akin to a gluttonous tick and created genuine fear that something might explode.

After the exam, I bee-lined for the market to refuel. I ate at the park, and recall lying on the ground under the shaded pathway, listening to nothing but the sound of trees alive in summer, the leaves dancing with the warm wind. Laying on the ground in silence was the quickest remedy to relief.

REASONS LAWYERS
FEEL LONELY

Stigmas → Legal Education

Analysis

Personality

Stressors

Expectations

Isolation

Training → Self-policing

Confidentiality

FEAR

Long work hours

Hypervigilence

Liv Ash

REALITY HITS
Indianapolis, Indiana
SEPTEMBER 2019

The walls we hit exist to save us from ourselves. Rather than obstacles, they protect us. They keep us from falling over the edge.

I failed the bar exam on my first attempt.

THE WORLD ISN'T SAFE
Houston, Texas

JANUARY 12, 2020

It was a trap; I was his prey; and too late I realized my predicament with no escape. Silence echoed the moment before it escalated.

His breath felt warm against my neck. Had it been a different man, at a different time, in a different setting—it may have been welcome. But it was not welcome. He was unwelcome.

I internally repeated: *Remain calm. Don't agitate him. Smile, laugh, make a joke. Maybe he'll get the point and walk away.* But he did not walk away, he persisted.

"Are you with that man over there?"

"No."

"Let's go talk to him."

My mind scrambled. What the hell did this guy want? The moment his energy strolled into the café, my senses heightened. He waltzed in wearing black slide sandals and socks, like he owned the hotel. He chatted loudly on his mobile phone. I saw him from the corner of my gaze approach the man with an accent who'd been in the elevator with me upon my arrival an hour earlier. The other guy was still there too. He'd also been present upon arrival, sitting by the door behind the column, wearing a faded yellow suit, with only a cell phone on the table within reach. He made me nervous; he devoured with his eyes.

I should have returned to my room after the sunset walk. But I didn't listen to that quiet voice whispering warning. I was happy to have felt sun on my face in early January and high on life from the endorphins of exercise and a visit to the art museum, despite an early morning flight. I wanted dinner, and then to call it a night. I purposefully sat in the middle of the sea of cobalt blue chairs, well away from the man who stared, my back to him so I could eat in peace.

Close to my face, he mumbled something in French. I couldn't make it out; my four years of high school French had rusted from two decades in storage. As he leaned in, speaking swiftly, I froze as my mind sprinted to keep up. I mumbled something back to him in French, hoping he would accept that I acknowledged his presence in my bubble, then leave.

He insisted I be "taken" by him to chat with the man who devoured with his eyes. My heart rate climbed. I instinctively stood upright. I hoped he—several inches shorter—would cease and desist. He did not.

He stepped closer, his breath at my chin, and said, "I like you."

The next instant, he reached for my phone and wallet; I parried, stretching my right arm across the table to block his acquisition. He saw his opening and seized his prey. Within a flash, we wrangled. He twisted my right arm inwardly and behind me, so that my body had to turn with him to my right. As he yanked my arm, pulling me towards the door, he repeated that we should talk to the man in the faded yellow suit. I dropped my body to lower my center of gravity, digging in for the battle.

I heaved backward, pulling my shoulder towards the bar behind me, and he resisted. He again yanked on my arm, and I responded with urgency. We tangled like this a few moments longer, warriors engaged in a tug-o-war for dominance of intent. Finally, I broke free. I righted myself and re-assessed the scene in a flash. *Am I safe? What just happened? Where is he?* He stumbled towards me laughing, yelling that I was a "queen," then demanded the young female employee get me a drink. She, like the two men, watched the struggle play out. No one assisted me. He further pressed her, and she barked back that the "lady didn't want a drink."

Survival responses are swift as lightning. Nothing prepares you for your body's innate mechanisms to defend and preserve life. The profundity of the moment and my body's response still astounds. Images flash in my mind's eye. I feel the warmth of his breath on my neck, and recall the apathy received by the onlookers: the young woman behind the bar; the man with an accent at the bar who watched; and the man in the yellow suit. He once again stared at me as I retreated to safety. As I walked by, he quipped, cool as a cucumber, "How are you tonight?" My blood ran cold at his blank, direct gaze. I bee-lined to the front desk and reported the incident. When I turned around, the yellow-suited man was gone.

Before the next morning's sunrise, I would restate the events on paper, to the police and firemen, and finally, the ER doctor. The police escorted the assailant, handcuffed, from the hotel. I called a friend I knew would be awake, in the hopes of receiving comfort. Yet she didn't seem shocked as I described his assault to my person. I asked her if a similar event happened to her. She said it happened often in college at parties, as if it was no big deal. With ice on my neck as I paced the hotel room, I said nothing in return to the disclosure, dumbfounded.

My neck and arm blazed, throbbing with anger as I watched the faces of first responders. Astonishment shook me at the unguarded apathy exhibited by front desk staff and police. A good cop/bad cop scene made for movies played out before me as I described with painful precision the assault, moment by moment. One cop dismissed me with his body language, the other regarded me with understanding. The most sensitive response to my shattered self came from a fireman. His face expressed sadness, his countenance a desire to protect. I won't forget in that moment how his understanding soothed my frenzied loneliness.

Once the ambulance arrived, I climbed in, and replayed an evening from twenty-one years earlier, with a similar response. I don't recall much about the journey towards the hospital after the policeman handed me a card with an incident number on it so I could check the website in the coming days. The city's response felt incredibly cold and mechanical.

I recall the taupe walls of the empty ER. I sat crying, alone in a foreign city at midnight, wearing a chartreuse cardigan to stave off the sterile chill. I received two shots of muscle relaxer in my neck to calm irritated nerves. The medical staff discharged me, and I scheduled an Uber back to the hotel. Glow from the streetlights filled the still night air as I watched them flash by in a daze.

WISDOM BUILDING
Indianapolis, Indiana

APRIL 2020

I failed the bar exam on my second attempt.

Exhausted and bewildered, I poured myself into my job. It's a lonely place, being left behind. Yet, I wasn't alone. Several colleagues also failed the bar exam on their first—and second—attempts. But it still feels lonely; I missed the proverbial "mark." I racked up $100,000 in student loan debt to earn a Doctorate in Law, and a test that doesn't measure the same variable from session to session determined my professional fate. Meanwhile, my head hurt, and sounds hurt worse. Because of SCCD, my brain struggled to decipher sounds and properly process stimuli. I chose to delay surgery, hoping I would pass the exam and then focus on healing. I struggled to iron out the wrinkles made by multiple, simultaneous sounds. And yet, I could hear the grinding of my own joints in my head.

I avoided situations that would "trip" my trigger. I stopped listening to music and attending concerts. The winter before, I left the symphony mid-program one cold evening because I could not endure the sounds of giggling children. During intermission, their innocent laughs pierced my temple like arrows. I exited the theater, tears streaking my makeup. I hiked up the hem of my dress, descended the marble stairs leading towards the atrium, and raced to the exit. The piercing pain was now crawling across my face, moving down my neck and into my shoulder. My face went numb before I made it to the car.

LAWYER MENTAL HEALTH

25% OF LAWYERS
REPORTED ELEVATED FEELINGS OF

→ INADEQUACY

→ ANXIETY

→ ISOLATION

→ DEPRESSION

→ INFERIORITY

→ ALIENATION

Liv Ash

A MEASURE OF RELIEF
Intensive Care Unit, Beech Grove, Indiana

MAY 23, 2020

Fluttering lids focused on the cupboards across the room. Quiet and softly lit, the peaceful room reflected a similar peace within my soul. I had never known such relaxation. And yet I was alone in the ICU only two months after COVID-19 burst upon humanity. Though I spoke with loved ones via phone as long as I could, there was no spouse or loved one to send me off like a ship to sea as they rolled me to an icy operating room. Likewise, no familiar smile warmed my heart upon awakening or held my hand in comfort.

But I wasn't alone. The nurse greeted me and inquired of my needs. I wanted water. I struggled to focus, and as my brain thawed from the effects of anesthesia, a surge of energy grew in my chest. Elation emblazoned my mind. The surgeon didn't mistakenly cut brain tissue causing permanent damage. Yet as swiftly as this energy arrived, it dissipated, and sleep rolled in like the tide.

The following day I leaped at the offer to "stroll" around the ICU. I wanted to move, to feel the solid earth beneath my feet. Masked and tethered by my waist to the nurse like a child to its parent at the park, I completed two laps before the reality of recovery beckoned. I walked away from that hospital heavier with the addition of a titanium screw in my skull, but lighter in spirit, humbled by the gift of new life. My road ahead meant wound healing, physical therapy, and the mother of all brain tests—my third attempt at the bar exam.

I know within my being that repairing the hole in my skull made reading and focusing less painful. One year after my first attempt, I passed the bar exam—only two months after cranial surgery. I had rested since surgery and wrangled Cluster Headache into submissive manageability, thanks to the serendipitous availability of a new medication. Standing alone in my cozy kitchen, I wept cleansing tears of gratitude and relief.

Though I planned to attend the First Friday art fair at the local coffee shop alone, I didn't feel lonely. I had achieved what I desired—and that gap between what I had and what I wanted was gone. An ebullience flowed, made better by a last-minute meet-up with a long-time friend and her husband. To celebrate passing the bar that night buoyed my soul. We had been friends for fifteen years—through jobs, crisis, childbirth, marriage, divorce, and graduate school. She had already met one of her life goals—to become a dentist. I celebrated this with her; now I was honored she celebrated with me.

LONELY HEARTS
Indianapolis, Indiana
AUTUMN 2020

Him: *I have been meaning to fix the rack that broke when you hung up the towel. I just fixed it and was hit with a profound sadness I have not felt in months. I am sitting on the stairs crying. I am sorry our dreams did not come to fruition; I blame myself for that. I am sorry I have broken your heart and saddened you. I love you and always will. Miss you terribly, but I know it is best to set you free and love you from afar forever.*

Me: *I love you.*

Him: *You will always be with me wherever I go. I truly love you; please never forget.*

Me: *I won't; I love you. I cried in the shower twice today. I miss you.*

Him: *I know how being lonely feels. It is a terrible feeling. Please don't go alone for long. Be happy and joyful. I don't want you feeling like this anymore. The thoughts going through my head are at times scary and awful. I don't want that for you. I love you too much to see you like that. I'm at the end and had an opportunity to be loved by you.*

LOSS

Indianapolis, Indiana

JANUARY 24, 2021

The absence of his presence creates an aching void in my soul.

CALCULATED SEPARATION

Indiana

EASTER 2021

I hate that feeling. Despite Herculean efforts, you can't dent their armor or influence their behavior. It's not your choice, and you must accept. It doesn't matter if you can defend your position with prosecutorial precision. It doesn't matter if you were "right" about the issue. It's still their choice to ignore you—to act as if you no longer exist. This calculated separation, the "silent treatment," is a form of emotional abuse. Disregard of a relationship is especially empty when the person who wields the sword of silence shares your DNA. The division lingers in memory like onions on your breath.

I know my heart; I know my motives. I will go to my grave settled in my soul, knowing my values and beliefs supported my behaviors. I advocated for the absent against verbal attacks of skewed hyperbole. When the inflammatory words turned towards me, I decided, in that instant, I would no longer accept berating. No longer would I deflect painful slights about my education, my emotions, and my body. It was a legacy moment, an event that fundamentally changed our relationship. I'd drawn a line in the sand, and it changed me. Decades of verbal jabs evaporated in the fire of spoken truth.

I attempted reconciliation. I poured out my heart on a video message— no reply. I tagged them in celebratory posts—no response. When I learned of it, I sent a text of condolence at their loss—yet still no acknowledgment. I replayed every flash of memory, minute by minute, analyzing my intent, behavior, and words. Three persons were present during that moment, and one is still bewildered by the continued ostracization. Estrangement is a palpable loneliness because it is not what I want for this relationship. Twenty years of birthday celebrations, holiday cards, and text messages froze in icy disregard.

This calculated separation is no longer worth my life energy. I grieve the positive memories. At one time, I looked up to this person. But I also accept that woven within those happy memories were many negative recollections. Cringeworthy, painful moments wherein my own and others' "weaknesses" were fodder for public humiliation at their hands.

How can a person profess a "WWJD" lifestyle yet repeatedly berate a relative? Such behavior fundamentally fails the foundations of Christianity, including the mantra to "love your neighbor as yourself." Perhaps it's because genuine self-love does not exist for this person. Perhaps it's because I stood my ground and would no longer permit bullying. To love another with *agape* love, we must first love ourself— with our foibles and gaping wounds. Whatever the motive for purposefully dissecting me from their life like a cancerous tumor, it's not, nor has it ever been, about me.

NO TURNING BACK
Indianapolis, Indiana

JULY 1, 2021

One minute, thirty-seven seconds. The left side of my neck ached as I craned, watching the numbers escalate. Reclined on the pelvic exam table, I stared at the humming machine that had just delivered electricity through a web of wiring, cauterizing my endometrium. That was quick.

I discussed options with my doctor, but I knew, and he knew I knew. I couldn't take hormones, and I refused to remove my uterus. The best option was ablation. I hoped it would eliminate the heavy, intermittent bleeding and pain. I had no intention of bearing a child. I was single, nearly forty-one years old, and in my first year working as an attorney. The "Goldilocks Zone" of my uterus was, by all data points, past its prime. I had multiple uterine fibroids, and imbalance wreaked havoc with my menstrual cycle. Each month brought a new form of abdominal torment and roller-coaster emotions; wicked cramps curling me into fetal position; and, most embarrassingly, breakthrough bleeding. It's as if I was once again a fourteen-year-old girl who forgot to pack a pad and had to tie her sweatshirt around her waist to avoid mortal embarrassment.

I wanted to be awake during the procedure; it was another life choice that, once made, was made for good. I understood the gravity of my decision: to remove the possibility of pregnancy and render my womb uninhabitable. The doctor honored this decision. During the post-operative appointment, however, he said, "I knew you were capable of being conscious during your ablation, so I wasn't worried about telling you that you could have been put under general anesthesia." I was surprised, but not angry. I would not have changed my mind. I'd been put under general anesthesia fourteen times already; I wanted to be awake for this one. He felt I was psychologically capable of being conscious and was mature enough to understand the risks and consequences of the decision. I felt *seen*.

Perhaps it's my upbringing, or years of managing pain, or multiple surgeries. Perhaps it's my personality. Whatever the mix, I want to be present and alert for big moments in life—the times that make us—the ones that stick with us and become a filter through which we process life and interact. These are the minutes you see emotion revealed, not veiled. Oftentimes, these are the hard things, the times when "shit gets real." And I want real.

In "real" times, we see the beautiful vulnerability of being human. And we don't waste energy acting as if we are not; we don't waste time being someone we don't know. On the contrary, it's in the real, big moments we discover who we are and what we want. What we learn in these times may cause pain. Yet we can work with the real, not build a house of cards that will topple when the next big moment arrives. Ablation was one of those moments. So was the morning I watched my neighbor wheeled away.

My bungalow sat directly across from his. I lived alone. He lived alone. The neighbors to my left and right also lived alone. Though I lived a stone's throw from them, we rarely spoke except a "Hello" or "Merry Christmas," yet I knew their routines. We never sat down to dinner together or shared a cold beverage on a humid summer evening. I wish I would have attempted to bring us together. The worst response would have been a "No."

I waved at him once or twice; I don't recall if we ever spoke. I do, however, recall with clarity details of that morning. Have you ever heard the cry of a loved one when they realize their family member is dead? It's awful. My heart ached for their loss. I was dumbstruck as I sat on my porch swing, watching the scene unfold. I was glued to the swing; I knew this was one of those big moments. It was a life-and-death moment, one that changed the lives of everyone involved, including me.

The police entered his home via the side door. They walked in and out a few times. His mother arrived, and then his sister. They approached the front door, opened it, and his sister wailed. I hear it even now. Mother restrained daughter at the sight of him on the floor, having taken his own life. She crumpled to the ground; tears poured from my eyes.

THE ART INSTITUTE: CONTEMPORARY GALLERY

Chicago, Illinois

APRIL 24, 2022

One week—I had one full week of work travel remaining before I drove the tangible evidence of my life 1,100 miles south for sunshine and space. Exhausted yet excited, I unpacked at the first hotel and nearly jogged the few blocks to the art museum. The beauty of art replenishes me, mind, body, and soul.

Nearing the end of my visit, making use of each minute before closing time, I climbed the flight of stairs to the contemporary gallery. Lost in the expansive canvases and bold colors before me, I sensed ease crawling back into my body as the pressures of packing released their grip on my chest. I could breathe in this quiet space of contemplation.

Not to be pushed aside too long, however, my mind turned towards the events of the first of two conferences. I reached for my phone and started the symphony of app opening and digital organizing. I noted the little red circle on a social media app and dutifully opened it to review. I read the message; confusion enveloped me. I reread it; my mind searched for an explanation.

Comprehension dawned. Immediately, I texted him a question; he called within a minute. With bulbous tears welling in my eyes, I descended the stairs and exited to the north. The temperate spring evening buzzed with life as pedestrians roamed the sidewalk. I found the quietest place I could and listened, pacing the pavement while endless tears evaporated from my hot cheeks.

I wrote two poems seven months later. The first blossomed after I spent time where I heal best—in nature. The second poem required more time to fully form, spurred by the catharsis of the preceding months and a stint of inner work and journaling. Healing through the loneliness of loss and crisis is not linear. Sometimes we celebrate the small wins before we release the deep-set wounds. Both are necessary to managing lonely feelings.

POEM YELLOW
by Olivia Ash

SOUTHWEST FLORIDA | AUGUST 29, 2022

The sweet smell of
sunbaked heather
soothes my weary soul.
I weep.
Not tears of sadness,
but of unspoken grief
breaching my heart,
erupting with delighted relief
into the expanse above.

MURDER OF A LOVE
by Olivia Ash

SOUTHWEST FLORIDA | NOVEMBER 20, 2022

Revelation stole my lung's breath with stunning swiftness.
I faltered, falling dangerously close to a faint.

The camel-colored cloth caught my weight as I dropped,
reverberating from my heart's shock.

The profundity of the moment brought tears to my eyes.
I stared through the veiled window.

Betrayal.
Purposeful deception.
I was duped.

My mind scrambled for comprehension.
Was it all lies?

Every memory of intimacy, laughter, and struggle
combusted to weightless ash in the revelation of his prior promise.

I grasped for words just out of reach.

Numbed, my body churned with vigor to protect my fractured soul.

The tears broiled, my heart iced, and anger flowed red with passionate fury.

An admission.
An apology.
A feeble attempt.

The arsenic death of a love evaporated before me as the shell of my soul wept bitter tears.

MANAGING LONELINESS

Notice your
environment.
Practice
mindfulness.

Ask
yourself
what you
need &
want in
life.

Talk it
out
with a
trusted
friend or
therapist.

Choose groups
of people who
share values &
interests.

Liv Ash

AT A LOSS
Southwest Florida

SUMMER 2022

I walked into my living room, rubbing my face to soothe the ache. I recall the beauty of the day as seen through the golden light cast by tangerine curtains. Tears formed. *Not again*, my heart sighed. I laid on the floor with renewed sadness. The knowing that comes through experience told me there would be more searching, more testing, and more surgery. *I want to share this, but who will understand? I'm tired of explaining.* The doctor's news overwhelmed my floundering emotional efforts to stay afloat. The dam fully burst, and tears rushed through, flooding my cheeks with salty sadness.

I wept bitterly that morning, a salty mix of anger and sadness. Only four months earlier, I moved my life across the country for sunshine and warmth to allow my aching body a break from months of dreary, gray skies and the cold of northern winters. The emotional toll of surgery after surgery created a storage shed of exhaustion corroding my body and outlook. I thought I was physically stable—that twenty years of surgeries were behind me.

As expected with the move, I missed my old neighborhood and its creative energy; I missed my friends. I loved my new home, yet struggled with the sometimes-lonely isolation inevitable in severing ties with the familiar while weaving new ones with the unfamiliar. Yet I knew I needed the change, space, and rest. I sighed, breathed deeply, then reassessed. Keep going, Liv.

FRACTURED
by Olivia Ash

SOUTHWEST FLORIDA | AUGUST 31, 2022

I promised myself I would do better,
BE better.
I would never react with such burning flame again.
I thought I had healed,
Put in the time and tears to become a better me.
Yet a look, a sigh, an accusatory word, and my work unravels.
What is wrong with me?
The wounded me is no more—but is she?
The unheard girl is still inside, tender, and vulnerable.
She aches for space to untie the knots.
What if I falter?
What if I fail?
What if I never reach "it?"
So be it.
I will keep going anyway.

HE SAID
by Olivia Ash

SOUTHWEST FLORIDA | OCTOBER 9, 2022

He said he loved the way my nose crinkled when I laughed.
I let him in.
He said he felt safe with me.
My heart softened.
He said he loved my shape.
I pulled him closer.
He caressed my hips.
I smelled his neck.
He said he loved me.
My heart said "Yes."

He said I would not hear from him.
I wrestled confusion.
He said he was not good enough.
I wondered, "Why?"
He said he didn't have "space" for me.
I cried.

He said he was ready.
My heart hesitated.
He said he would be there.
I never sought his support.

He said he wanted me.
I listened behind my wall.
He said he loved me.
My heart sobbed.

He said the journey was hard.
My body applauded agreement.
He said he was sorry.
I sat a cynic.
He said he had grown.
I faltered to trust.
He said he loved me.
I let his words drop.

He said…
He said…
He said…

REGULATE & REASSESS
The porch swing, Southwest Florida, 5:46 p.m.

OCTOBER 29, 2022

On September 28, 2022, Hurricane Ian brought catastrophic damage to Ft. Myers, Cape Coral, and surrounding Florida regions. My home sits less than four miles east of Matlacha Islands, northwest of Cape Coral. Residents suffered great loss, including the washing away of several homes and businesses. The hurricane hit five months after my cross-country relocation and renovation of my home. Though it had been a short time, seedlings of social connection were growing. I remembered familiar faces and made efforts to engage with locals on the island. Witnessing the catastrophic damage to their property and way of life brought tears to my eyes.

While Ian devastated the region and left residents with a profound sense of loss and loneliness, the shared trial strengthened the community. In the aftermath, I met many neighbors who offered help as I, a single woman living alone, picked up the debris of my home damaged by the hurricane. Their outpouring of assistance warmed my heart. I won't forget the experience. The following poem is the output of intentional efforts to process emotions through the practice of mindfulness—a proven strategy to reduce loneliness. Mindfulness is "attending to one's present moment with purpose and kindness" and without judgment. It's a simple, yet powerful, tool to reframe perspective whenever life requires it.

THEA WINS
by Olivia Ash

The whistle of a western
breeze alerts my senses.
The warm wind whips 'round broken pines,
purifying the feeble forest.
An aviary celebration
heralds the dawn of new life,
among the barren aftermaths
of Poseidon's fury.
She's there, ever present,
bestowing her glistening glow,
inviting every being to begin again,
even if her rays merely warm wounded bones.

VALENTINE'S DAY
by Olivia Ash

SOUTHWEST FLORIDA | FEBRUARY 14, 2023

Feelings are fleeting.
Seasons come and go.
We live and lose.
Anger dissipates.

Open your eyes.
Breathe deeply.
Radically accept.
Nurture hope.

Love.
Love.
Love.

YOU SAY TO ME
by Olivia Ash

SOUTHWEST FLORIDA | JULY 18, 2023

You say to me, "You deserve it."
Yet I feel embarrassment and shame.
No human deserves anything, or do all humans deserve everything?

You say to me, "You're intimidating."
And I feel confusion and shame.
Should I be less of me to appease?

Am I worthy because I exist?

Am I intimidating because my presence stokes their internal fears?

At what point did I learn my worth is what I earned and merited?

When did I learn to earn love and restrain my being so you could feel better?

Say instead what you mean:
I deserve because I am suitable, perhaps because I've earned it.
And you feel intimidated because who I am illuminates your own self esteem.

I feel misunderstood.
I feel lonely.

TIPS TO EASE LONELINESS

- Connect with others.
- Learn a new skill.
- Break up your routine.
- Vary work tasks.
- Examine your values.
- Write down your _needs_.
- Write down your _wants_.
- Mentor or volunteer.
- Name problems.
- Know: we all feel _loneliness_.

LIV ASh

MY BEST ADVOCATE

Southwest Florida

PRESENT DAY

Twenty-four years since the fire of anger burned within my youthful heart as I wept bitter tears of loss lying in my dorm room, I face painful new physical symptoms and more testing.

I tend my body imperfectly, but consistently. I tolerate pain. I "fight through it" and "get the job done." These questionably injurious colloquialisms were drilled into my psyche via years of competition. I pursue to achieve. Doctors seem perplexed when they meet me, surprised at rare diagnoses that don't visually align with expectations. I wonder whether the dichotomy between what doctors see and test results weakens their sense of urgency.

When people learn I juggle multiple rare conditions and carry the scars from a laundry list of surgeries, they expect whining and wallowing—in short, visible weakness. Yet I make daily efforts to remain as healthy as ability will allow. I want to live what life I have left! Few understand why I keep going when the easier path would be to remain immobile, feeding on medication. I still function *despite* chronic disease *because* I move daily. Too often, however, I hear phrases such as, "You don't look like you've had so many surgeries. No one could tell you're falling apart. I don't know how you do it; I would be a mess."

And then, instead of dropping the topic, or practicing empathy by holding space, I receive the opposite. Tact evaporates, and insecurity shoves kindness to the ground: "At least you're tall, thin, and pretty. I wish I had your waist. You look better than me, and I don't have your excuses." And my least favorite, "You should be grateful; you've got good genes." *Sigh.* Ignorant, insensitive statements. I do have *some* good genes; I also inherited faulty ones. It requires immense energy to mitigate negative consequences of their expression. Comments like these annoy and exhaust me. They breed loneliness if I let them. However, I've learned not to play the game. I've learned to let go of some relationships and practice mindful solitude. I've learned to advocate my case in the face of assumed disbelief.

Yet, I struggle with balance. I may have the drive of the Energizer Bunny, but my body has an expiration date. Years of consistent pressure, like water against a dam, are cracking my physical foundations. Unexpectedly, my vision blurs, eyelid twitches, and face begins to numb. Sometimes, I turn over in bed and the room rocks. Sometimes, my ears ring and hearing fades for up to a minute. It's as if a musician struck a triangle within my ear canal; the piercing sound is all I hear, and then it dissipates into silence, taking life energy with it. Once hearing returns, I'm left with an aching ear and irritable disposition. These episodes come quickly, fade slowly, and recur multiple times a day. I experience intermittent nausea and dizziness. I live with an incessant, aching pressure at the base of my skull.

When pain is an ever-present, unsolicited "plus one," you learn its personality and habits. And when behaviors change, as they do with people, you know something's up. The cranial surgery in 2020 was successful, but not for long. I once again have a hole in the thin bone that separates my brain from my inner ear. This is unexpected and its cause unknown. The timing, intensity, and nature of this pain is different. After conversations with experts, I am doing what I can to maintain blood pressure and stave off dizzy spells. A genetics test confirmed a mutation in a collagen gene—the implications unknown. I do not like to take medications, yet sometimes they are necessary to give my hypervigilant body a break from the pressure that pounds at the base of my skull.

Chronic pain is incessant in its urgency and relentless in its pursuit of acknowledgment. So is loneliness. It's easy to marinate in the muck of mounting losses. However, in two decades of managing, I've learned to appreciate the present more mindfully, so I lose less precious life energy. This is one way I practice mindfulness to manage lonely feelings, especially when my temple aches from Cluster Headache and I feel no one understands. I have become a better listener when pain and loneliness seek an audience. This permits me to learn the character of pain and what loneliness is telling me I need. It's an imperfect science. Yet, like the scientific method, by conversing, observing, and questioning, I have improved my self-care choices for both body and mind.

Living is a lonely road at times because even our relatives, friends, or chosen family cannot know our innermost desires and despairs unless we share. And even if we find the courage to speak, our feelings may not be received as hoped. How do we tell our closest people that it's a tenuous balancing act to simply get out of bed some days because throbbing pain in your temple is on the other side of opening your eyes? We do it anyway.

We share without expectation. It's easier said than done. But by learning with whom we are treated gently without judgment, and sharing anyway, we begin to feel understood. And this is key to managing loneliness. The more understood we feel, the less lonely we feel. It's an inverse relationship. Conversely, the less understood we feel, the greater the loneliness. We must choose each day how we will show up in life.

The next big choice is choosing with whom we share that precious life energy.

My medical conditions are rare, and few persons truly understand the pains I manage and the effort to keep going. I know this. However, this reality creates a loneliness that ebbs and flows in my life. It's stronger on days when pain brings me to tears or I haven't made time to create and socialize. It's worse when I've isolated myself. I'm learning it's okay to wish I didn't have to manage consistent pains. But that's not reality, so I've learned to treat myself more gently on hard days, to make time to do what brings me joy, and reach out to my support network.

Finding social support is critical. Whether blood relatives or chosen ones, making time to be with, relate with, and learn from others is critical to managing loneliness. If you have a non-existent network, the best place to begin forming one is with you. Managing loneliness is about navigating the space between. This space is ever-shifting, just as each morning's sky brings a new canvas. We start with what we have. Then, we assess what we need and desire. Last, we make efforts to adjust both so that we close that gap.

I've grown in wisdom, tempering my inner fire. Perseverance is built through trials, pain, and sometimes deep loneliness. It's persistence, despite difficulty or delay to achieve. It's not easy, and often messy. I'm still learning to pause, practice patience, and press on. I've allowed loss, crisis, personal shortcomings, and weak social support to teach me that I am my best advocate. I am committed to my purpose while speaking my voice, despite chances I lose. I am responsible for teaching myself about myself. In doing so, I better represent my wants and needs, and no longer explain myself to those not living in my body. I've accepted that chronic pain and loneliness are a part of living.

Mark Twain is credited for saying, "Courage is not the absence of fear, it's acting in spite of it." Building resilience is a process. I call this quality "bouncebackability." It is a ceaseless process of positively adapting to challenging life experiences by adjusting our behaviors to demands. Some days, pain is unbearable, and the void of loneliness swells. In these moments, I step away from my desk, lay on the floor, and weep frustrated tears. Then I move along. Other days, I am overwhelmed with gratitude as the sun shines warm on my face, and I cry thankful tears. As I watch the clouds color crimson at sunset, my perspective shifts: I am aware; I have choice. Emotions come. Emotions flow. Emotions go.

There's an amazing clarity that comes with settled choice. The journey, though, is fraught with indecision and struggle. *You cannot come against yourself.* I've not given up on me because I'm my most reliable advocate. I know me better than anyone else on the planet. To best learn, I question, listen, and apply. Understanding will flow. Self-compassion will grow. I know my heart and learn blind spots. I know which parts of me require strengthening. As time passes, I release the need for approval from the crowd or their assessment of the veracity or intensity of my life experiences.

When aches agitate or the iron walls of loneliness constrict, I rely on my own heart and mind to assess and reset my narrative. I remind myself to seek social support. But I don't feel sorry for myself. I ache for losses, yet don't regret my choices. I still laugh. I love with purpose. I seek, sense, and share beauty. Beauty is shown to lessen pain; permit learning and growth; and foster creation.

Becoming my best advocate means not acting against myself. Applying this principle is imperfect, and retreat is sometimes necessary. But I continue the journey when I've regulated, reassessed, and am ready to relate. When fatigued, I remember that I put in the grueling work of learning to love myself through pain and loneliness. Not to advocate for myself would be a disservice. Remaining in unhealthy relationships would be a disservice. By learning, loving, and living my truth, I speak volumes without uttering a word, and loneliness quiets.

Time and gravity are constants—one pulls us forward, the other pulls us towards. I know our machinations fail in the fire of time. Eventually, despite my efforts to listen, apply, and grow, my body will give up the ghost and finally rest. Until then, and with the knowledge that this is our shared ultimate destination, I choose daily to look into the mirror and decide how to best use experience as my teacher. In doing so, I don't merely exist, I Liv.

RESOURCES

DOCUMENTS:

Olivia Ash & Peter H. Huang, *Loneliness in COVID-19, Life, and Law*, 32 Health Matrix 55 (2022).
Available at: https://scholarlycommons.law.case.edu/healthmatrix/vol32/iss1/5

Office of the U.S. Surgeon General, *Our Epidemic of Loneliness and Isolation. The U.S. Surgeon General's Advisory on the Healing Effects of Social Connection and Community*, 2023. Available at: https://www.hhs.gov/sites/default/files/surgeon-general-social-connection-advisory.pdf

PODCASTS:

The Opportunity in Loneliness with Wellness Expert and Loneliness Researcher, Olivia Ash, We Should Talk About That Podcast, originally aired July 11, 2022. Available at: https://www.westatpod.com/episodes/episode/7db1f18b/the-opportunity-in-loneliness-with-wellness-expert-and-loneliness-researcher-olivia-ash

Vivek Murthy, *To Be a Healer*, On Being with Krista Tippett, originally aired April 13, 2023. Available at: https://onbeing.org/programs/vivek-murthy-to-be-a-healer/

WEBSITES:

#AloneTogether. Available at: https://www.alonetogether.com/

Crisis Text Line. Available at: Crisis Text Line | Text HOME To 741741 free, 24/7 Crisis Counseling

The Institute for Well-Being in Law. Available at: https://lawyerwellbeing.net/resources-2/

Loneliness Research, Liv Balanced, LLC. Available at: https://www.livbalanced.net/loneliness

Social Connection, Office of the U.S. Surgeon General. Available at: https://www.hhs.gov/surgeongeneral/priorities/connection/index.html

ENDNOTES

1. Emily Dickinson, *Collected Poems*, published by Barnes & Noble, Inc. 1993; originally published in 1924 as *The Complete Poems of Emily Dickinson*, page 6.

2. Emily Dickinson, T*he Loneliness One dare not sound 777*, Available at: https://allpoetry.com/The-Loneliness-One-dare-not-sound

3. Neil Burton, M.D., *What Are Basic Emotions?* Psychology Today, Jan. 7, 2016. Available at: https://www.psychologytoday.com/us/blog/hide-and-seek/201601/what-are-basic-emotions

4. Catherine Barnett, *On Emily Dickinson*. Poetry Society of America, 2023 Available at: https://poetrysociety.org/poems-essays/old-school/catherine-barnett-on-emily-dickinson

5. Definition of "soul" 2023, Available at: https://www.dictionary.com/browse/soul

6. Definition of "horror" 2023, Available at: https://www.dictionary.com/browse/horror

7. *Id.*

8. Shawn Achor et al., *America's Loneliest Workers, According to Research*, HARV.BUS.REV. (Mar.19, 2018), https://hbr.org/2018/03/americas-loneliest-workers-according-to-research [https://perma.cc/MHK8-NVP7].

9. Olivia Ash and Peter H. Huang, *Loneliness in COVID-19, Life*,

and Law, 32 Health Matrix 55 (2022). Available at: https://scholarlycommons.law.case.edu/healthmatrix/vol32/iss1/5

10. *Adverse Possession* by Olivia Ash, an essay within the *Deserts to Mountaintops Anthology*, Soul Speak Press, pp. 293 – 312, January 25, 2023.

11. Ash, *supra* note 9, at 62.

12. *Id.* at 61.

13. Office of the U.S. Surgeon General, *Our Epidemic of Loneliness and Isolation. The U.S. Surgeon General's Advisory on the Healing Effects of Social Connection and Community*, 2023, page 9. Available at: https://www.hhs.gov/sites/default/files/surgeon-general-social-connection-advisory.pdf

14. *Id.*

15. *See* Office, *supra* note 13, at 7.

16. Self-love Journal, Switch Research, Inc., 2021, page 18.

17. Olivia Ash, *Ask & Act* Worksheet, Liv Balanced, LLC., 2021.

18. Switch, *supra* note 16, at 18.

19. John G. McGraw, *God, and the Problem of Loneliness*, 28 RELIGIOUS STUDIES. 319, 331 (1992).

20. Achor, *supra* note 8.

21. Ash, *supra* note 9, at 91.

22. Spoken by Edward Rochester Fairfax to Jane Eyre in the film *Jane Eyre*, Focus Features and Universal Pictures, 2011.

23. Rossi P, Little P, De La Torre ER, Palmaro A. *If you want to understand what it really means to live with cluster headache, imagine... fostering empathy through European patients' own stories of their experiences.* Funct Neurol. 2018 Jan/Mar; 33(1):57-59. doi: 10.11138/fneur/2018.33.1.057. PMID: 29633698; PMCID: PMC5901943.

AUTHOR BIO

OLIVIA ASH, ESQ., MS

Olivia (Liv) Ash is an Indiana-licensed attorney, health educator, and founder of Liv Balanced, LLC. She's a published author and award-winning researcher on loneliness. Liv speaks to businesses about integrating well-being practices to manage mental health. She's been invited to present her research to Stanford Law School and conducted seminars for the American Bar Association; the International Society for Research on Emotion; Indiana University; the Institute for Well-Being in Law; and the Wellness Council of Indiana. Liv's been featured on podcasts and within articles discussing well-being. Learn more about loneliness and Liv's current projects by visiting https://www.livbalanced.net.

ACKNOWLEDGMENTS

When asked if I wanted an "Acknowledgments" page for this book, I replied, "Yes, but I need to think on it." I ruminated, and returned to this: I cannot express in one page the depth of gratitude to those who have contributed measures to the symphony that is this memoir. Listing persons' names with a short note feels insufficient and crosses into territory I've reserved for myself. To this end, I will thank each soul when the time is appropriate. However, I am honored by the kindness of strangers and grateful for the support of friends and family. As time passes, my appreciation for the depth of support received during a time of intense focus will grow. To each person whose life energy mingled with mine, whether briefly or for a season, thank you. Writing this book was my task alone, yet I know I was—and am—supported.

www.ingramcontent.com/pod-product-compliance
Lightning Source LLC
Chambersburg PA
CBHW031521120626
46545CB00005B/1942